Letters to a
Young Teacher

Other Books by Jonathan Kozol

Letters to a
Young Teacher

Jonathan Kozol

THREE RIVERS PRESS
NEW YORK

Copyright © 2007 by Jonathan Kozol

Published in the United States by Three Rivers Press,
an imprint of the Crown Publishing Group,
a division of Random House, Inc., New York.
www.crownpublishing.com

Three Rivers Press and the Tugboat design are registered
trademarks of Random House, Inc.

Originally published in hardcover in the United States by
Crown Publishers, an imprint of the Crown Publishing Group,
a division of Random House, Inc., New York, in 2007.

Library of Congress Cataloging-in-Publication Data
Kozol, Jonathan.
     Letters to a young teacher / Jonathan Kozol.
          p.   cm.
     1. Teaching—United States. 2. Teachers—United States—
     Anecdotes. 3. Teaching—United States—Anecdotes.
     I. Title.
     LB1776.2.K69   2007
     371.1—dc22   2007002689

ISBN 978-0-307-39372-2

Printed in the United States

Design by Barbara Sturman

10 9 8 7 6 5 4 3 2 1

First Paperback Edition

For Francesca

and for all those other
teachers, young in age
or young at heart, who
come into our classrooms
with a love for children and
a thirst for justice

TO THE READER

The letters in this little book were written to a first grade teacher I will call Francesca who, after she had taken a position at an inner-city school in Boston, soon began to write to me, as many teachers do, and invited me to visit in her classroom.

In order to include some of the issues raised by other teachers in whose classes I have visited or who have written to me on a friendly impulse, as Francesca did, I have expanded the scenario from time to time by incorporating some of their experience into my portrayal of Francesca. I have also disguised a number of the details of Francesca's situation, including certain biographical matters and time factors that might otherwise invade her privacy in ways that I believe would be unfair to her.

Francesca, however, is a very real and wonderful young person who is also an astute observer of the politics of education and who, in her conversations and her correspondence with me, proved to be a shrewd, sometimes irreverent, and persistent questioner. Some of her questions forced me to reach back into my own career and to unearth almost forgotten memories. On occasion, this has led me to restate an incident or conversation from one of the other books I've written about children in the course of 40 years. I'd like to thank Francesca for impelling me to share these memories with her, even when they sometimes painfully remind me of mistakes I've made, either in the classroom as a teacher or, in later years, in efforts to resist a public policy or practice I thought damaging to students.

Most of all, I want to thank her for the favor she has given me in making me feel welcome in her class and—by her willingness to speak with candor of the challenges she's faced—bringing me so very close to the immediate and day-by-day concerns of those who, like herself, have chosen to devote their lively spirits and their deepest ethical ideals to the education of our children.

—Byfield, Massachusetts, April 2007

Letters to a
Young Teacher

CHAPTER ONE

A Life Among
Schoolchildren

Dear Francesca,

I was very happy that you wrote to me and I apologize for taking two weeks to reply. I was visiting schools in other cities in the first part of the month and I didn't have a chance to read your letter carefully until tonight.

The answer to your question is that I would love to come and visit in your classroom and I'm glad that you invited me. I'd also like to reassure you that you didn't need to worry that I'd think your letter was presumptuous. I like to hear from teachers and, as you have probably suspected, I feel very close to quite a few of them, especially the ones who work with little children in the elementary grades, because those are the grades I used to teach. I think that teaching is a beautiful profession and that teachers of young children do one of the best things that there is to do in life: bring joy and beauty, mystery and mischievous delight into the hearts of little people in their years of greatest curiosity.

Sometimes when I'm visiting a school, a teacher whom I may have met once when she was in college, or with whom I may have corresponded briefly, or a teacher whom I've never met but who's read one of my books and feels as if she knows me, sees me standing in the corridor and comes right up and tells me, "Come and visit in my classroom!" Sometimes she doesn't give me any choice. She simply grabs me by the arm and brings me to the classroom. Then, when I get there, typically she puts me on the spot and asks if I would like to teach a lesson or ask questions to her children.

I love it when teachers let me do this, but I almost always do it wrong at first, because it's been a long time since I was a teacher, and I often ask the kind of question that gets everybody jumping from their seats and speaking out at the same time. Six-year-olds, when they become excited, as you put it in your letter, have "only a theoretical connection with their chairs." They do the most remarkable gymnastics to be sure you see them. A little girl sitting right in front of me will wave her fingers in my face, climbing halfway out of her chair, as if she's going to poke me in the eyes if I won't call on her, and making the most heartrending sounds—"Ooooh! Ooooh! Ooooh! Ooooh!"—in case I still don't notice that she's there.

Then, when I finally call on her, more often than not she forgets the question that I asked, looks up at me in sweet bewilderment, and asks me, "What?" It turns out she didn't have a thing to say. She just wanted me to recognize that she was there.

The teacher usually has to bail me out. She folds her arms and gives the class one of those looks that certain teachers do so well, and suddenly decorum is restored.

It's a humbling experience, but I think that it's a good one too, for someone who writes books on education to come back into the classroom and stand up there as the teacher does day after day and be reminded in this way of what it's like to do the real work of a teacher. I sometimes think that every education writer, every would-be education expert, and every politician who pontificates, as many do so condescendingly, about the "failings" of the teachers in the front lines of our nation's public schools ought to be obliged to come into a classroom once a year and teach the class, not just for an hour with the TV cameras watching but for an entire day, and find out what it's like. It might at least impart some moderation to the disrespectful tone with which so many politicians speak of teachers.

In my writings through the course of nearly 40 years, I have always tried to bring the mighty and ferocious educational debates that dominate the pages of the press and academic publications, in which the voices of our teachers are too seldom heard, back from the distant kingdom of intimidation and abstraction—lists of "mandates," "sanctions," and "incentives" and "performance standards" and the rest—into the smaller, more specific world of colored crayons, chalk erasers, pencil sharpeners, and tiny quarrels, sometimes tears and sometimes uncontrollably contagious jubilation of which daily life for a real teacher and her students is, in fact, composed.

I'm often disappointed, when I visit some of the allegedly sophisticated schools of education, to recognize how very little of the magic and the incandescent chemistry that forms between a truly gifted teacher and her children is conveyed to those who are about to come into our classrooms. Many of these schools of education have been taken over, to a troubling degree, by people who have little knowledge of the classroom but are the technicians of a dry and mechanistic, often business-driven version of "proficiency and productivity." State accountability requirements, correlated closely with the needs and wishes of the corporate community, increasingly control the ethos and the aims of education that are offered to the students at some of these schools.

But teachers, and especially the teachers of young children, are not servants of the global corporations or drill sergeants for the state and should never be compelled to view themselves that way. I think they have a higher destiny than that. The best of teachers are not merely the technicians of proficiency; they are also ministers of innocence, practitioners of tender expectations. They stalwartly refuse to see their pupils as so many future economic units for a corporate society, little pint-sized deficits or assets for America's economy, into whom they are expected to pump "added value," as the pundits of the education policy arena now declaim. Teachers like these believe that every child who has been entrusted to their care comes into their classroom with *inherent* value to begin with.

Many of the productivity and numbers specialists who have rigidified and codified school policy in recent years do not seem to recognize much preexisting value in the young mentalities of children and, in particular, in children of the poor. Few of these people seem to be acquainted closely with the lives of children and, to be as blunt as possible about this, many would be dreadful teachers because, in my own experience at least, they tend to be rather grim-natured people who do not have lovable or interesting personalities and, frankly, would not be much fun for kids to be with.

A bullying tone often creeps into their way of speaking. A cocksure overconfidence, what Erik Erikson described as "a destructive conscientiousness," is not unfamiliar too. The longer they remain within their institutes of policy or their positions in the government, the less they seem to have a vivid memory of children's minuscule realities, their squirmy bodies and their vulnerable temperaments, their broken pencil points, their upturned faces when the teacher comes and leans down by their desk to see why they are crying.

I suspect that you and I will come back to this matter many times. For now I simply want to say I'm very, very glad you're teaching here in Boston, because that means that I can visit sometimes in your class without needing to make plans long in advance. Thank you for saying it's okay if I stop by one day without much prior warning, which makes things a whole lot easier for me. As you know, you're teaching in the neighborhood where I began to teach, so I definitely will *not* need to ask you for directions!

I promise to visit as soon as I can. Meanwhile, I hope the next few weeks are not too intimidating for you. You said you like your principal and that she's been kind to you. That's one big victory to start with. I'm sure there will be many more during the weeks ahead. In spite of the butterflies you said are making "many, many loop-the-loops" within your stomach almost every morning as you head for school, try hard to enjoy this first month with your children if you can.

It will someday be a precious memory.

CHAPTER TWO

Establishing the Chemistry

First Days in the Classroom

Dear Francesca,

You asked me how I felt the first day that I ever taught within a public school.

The truthful answer is that I was terrified, even more than you were, I suspect, because I'd had no preparation as a teacher. I had gone to Harvard College, where I was a literature major, then had studied briefly as a Rhodes Scholar in England and had lived in Paris, where I'd studied writing in the company of older writers who were living there.

When I came back to the United States in 1964 and decided I would like to teach in public school, I knew nothing about teaching and had never had a class in education. But my lack of qualifications didn't seem to matter to officials in the Boston Public Schools, who were so desperate to hire almost anyone who would agree to teach in one of Boston's poorest neighborhoods that my application was approved without much questioning.

I found myself, within three weeks, assigned to teach a fourth grade class in Roxbury, the section of the city where the black community of Boston was confined to live, a pattern of confinement, as you've noted, that exists unaltered to the present day.

My school was in a ghostly looking, badly overcrowded, and physically decrepit building where my students couldn't even be provided with a classroom of their own. We had to share an undivided auditorium with 35 other children in another fourth grade class, and with a choral group, and sewing class (fifth grade girls, all black, were taken out of academic classes for an hour every day to learn to sew on old machines like those my grandmothers had used), and with a group rehearsing almost all fall for a Christmas play that somehow never was produced.

One windy afternoon that fall, a rotted frame of windows in our make-shift class collapsed. I was standing close enough to catch the frame before the glass could shatter on the children sitting just beneath it.

Some of the children seemed to have accepted these conditions or, at least, did not appear to feel they had the right to question them. Others did not suffer these indignities so passively but seemed to simmer with hostility toward many of the teachers and the principal. When the anger of these kids erupted, they were taken to the basement of the school, where whippings were administered by an older teacher who employed a rattan whip which he first dipped in vinegar in order to intensify the pain that it inflicted on a child's outstretched hands. The year before, one of the students in my class landed in the hospital after one of several whippings he'd received. His right forefinger had been permanently distorted as a consequence.

In the spring, the principal assigned me to another fourth grade class that had a classroom of its own but was in an even worse condition than the class in which I had begun, because the children in that room had had a string of substitute teachers almost the entire year. In the course of the preceding months, twelve different teachers had appeared and disappeared.

One of the most unhappy of these teachers, an emotionally unstable person who had no experience in teaching and an oddly frenzied look within his eyes, seemed to be a kindly man, but he could not control the pent-up anger of the children. One very cold day he made the bad mistake of stepping outside on the platform of the fire escape to clap the chalk erasers. One of the children slammed the door shut while he was outside. He banged on the door and shouted warnings at the children, but they wouldn't let him in. A teacher, alerted by the noise, who came into the room at last, said that he was red in the face and stamping his feet—"like Rumpelstiltskin!" in her words—until she opened the door to rescue him.

That was his last day at the school. Seven additional substitute teachers came and went during the next ten days. At that point, the principal told me this would be my class for the remainder of the year.

As you can imagine, I began my first day with those children with the deepest trepidation. I knew how angry and distrustful they'd become—rightfully so, in view of all the damage that the school had done to them by now. But I also knew it was essential for me to suppress the self-doubts I was feeling and do something, anything I could contrive, to give the kids the confidence that a new beginning had been made.

It wasn't easy at the start. I literally had to shout the children down during the first few days in order to be heard. I think they were shocked by this, because I'd worked with some of them in small groups earlier that year, and they'd never heard me raise my voice like that before.

Once the class calmed down a bit, I sat on my desk and made a promise to the children: I told them that they would not be abandoned. I told them I was there to stay. I don't know why it is that they believed me. They had no reason to accept such promises from yet another teacher. I do know that, from that point on, I did my damnedest to exploit every bit of personal theatricality I had at my disposal in order to infuse that room with energy and, as best I could, with the exhilaration that might bring some smiles to the very sullen faces that had come to be their adaptation to conditions that most children, rich or poor, in any school or district would have found unbearable.

Francesca, I don't want you to imagine that I was immediately successful. There are too many stories about "super-teachers" who walk into hopeless situations and work instant miracles. Those stories make good movies but don't often happen in real life; and I know that, in my own case anyway, I did not work any miracles that spring. Some of the kids remained resistant to me for a long, long time, and there were two or three who never really opened up to me until the last weeks of the year. But I did discover—and I still don't understand the chemistry that made this happen—that most of the children seemed to trust me, and one reason for this, I believe, is that they could see that I did not condemn them for the chaos and confusion they'd been through, because I told them flatly that they had been treated in a way that I thought unforgivable.

Then, too, because I've always had a tendency to say exactly what I think to children, but to do it in a way that isn't too discouraging and gloomy, trying always to extract some kind of humor or sense of absurdity out of a situation that appears like an impossible calamity, I think most of the children actually got to like me, which, as in the case of almost any first-year teacher, is the kind of unexpected blessing that we pray for.

In the Boston schools in those days, there was a

prescribed curriculum, not unlike those lists of standards, lesson plans, and day-by-day instructions that are given to the teachers in most inner-city schools today. Obedience to rules and orders was a constant emphasis in all of these materials. Teachers were provided with a list of notable quotations which we were to post on bulletin boards, or read aloud, or have our students memorize: "He who would command others must first learn to obey. . . . The first law that ever God gave to man was a law of obedience. . . . True obedience is true liberty. . . . Every day in every way it is our duty to obey. . . . Obedience sums up our entire duty."

The phonics text I was supposed to use was a basal reader in which there were no black characters. There were a couple of illustrations in the book in which the faces of the characters were lightly tanned, which may have been a timid nod to racial sensibilities, but the stories in the book had no connection to the lives of anyone who was not white and middle class. The antiquated social studies textbook I was given by a woman who was called "the master teacher" for the fourth grade classes in the school, an overtly racist publication, portrayed the people of Africa as "savage and uncivilized. . . . Their skins are of so dark a brown color that they almost look black. Their noses are large and flat. Their lips are thick. Their eyes are black and shining. . . . Their hair is so curly that it seems like wool. They are Negroes and they belong to the black race." Of the children of Switzerland, by comparison, the textbook said, "These children are handsome. Their eyes are blue. Their hair is golden yellow. Their white skins are clear, and their cheeks are as red as ripe, red apples."

The first thing I did was to rip down from the walls and blackboards all of these materials—"obedience" quotations and the rest—and to stash the social studies textbooks in a box and seal it shut and stuff it in the closet. Then, drawing mostly on my own delights and memories, I tacked up prints of paintings by Joan Miró and Paul Klee and brought in some records of French children's songs, and some calming music by Schuman, Ravel, and Brahms.

Again, drawing on my own experience from college days and from the years I'd spent in Europe, I introduced a few familiar poems of Robert Frost, some early lyrical poems of William Butler Yeats, and some beautiful posters of the streets of Paris and its skyline, and a map of Paris too, which became of special interest to the children when I told them I had lived there and showed them the street on which I'd lived.

I ultimately ditched a set of horrible lesson plans in social studies I'd been given and did a unit about Paris, which included measuring distances, calculating costs of buying food at small cafés, and other elements of daily life within a city I knew well enough to make it something of a geographical adventure for the children.

As I said, I can't pretend that all of this was magically successful. I certainly would not propose that any of these amateurish efforts on my part ought to be considered "innovative models" for another generation of beginning teachers. I simply wanted to begin by teaching things I knew and loved and felt that I could talk about with genuine excitement, since I thought—and this turned out to be the case—that my own enthusiasm might well prove to be contagious.

The children, to be honest, never took to Miró, but one of the paintings of Paul Klee, which is called "Bird Garden," was an instant favorite and it caused a pile-up of bodies every time the children had a chance to file past it on the way to recess or when they were lining up before dismissal. The art instructor at the school told me that she thought a painter like Paul Klee was too sophisticated for the children of this neighborhood. I didn't argue with her, but I think the children in my classroom proved her expectations to be incorrect.

I won't go into any greater detail now about the various changes that I made to try to bring some optimism about learning to those 35 fourth graders whose achievement levels had been knocked flat by the time I came into their room. (Only seven were reading and writing at grade level when I came into the class. Nearly a third were still at second grade level. I had to figure out a way to deal with this as an immediate emergency.) The point for now is not to give a breakdown of the strategies I tried but to respond to the familiar questions—"What do you *do*? How do you break through the lethargy you find?"—that teachers ask me when they come into a classroom where the spirits of the children seem to have been bludgeoned into dull passivity by previous months or years of instability.

Most teachers, fortunately, do not come into situations quite as awful as the one that I encountered, but many have described to me conditions that are only slightly less horrendous. They also tell me—and this is the case not only with those teachers who have entered education on a "fast-track" program that sends them into urban schools with only a few weeks of preparation, but also with those teachers who've attended schools of education—that they have been given almost no advice at all on strategies for breaking through that first and frozen moment of encounter with a class that has already undergone the kind of pedagogic battering my students had experienced before I was assigned to them.

"Start out tough and stick to the prescribed curriculum," new teachers are too frequently advised. This, in my belief, is the worst possible advice. Establishing a chemistry of trust between the children and ourselves is a great deal more important than to charge into the next three chapters of the social studies text or packaged reading system we have been provided: the same one that was used without success by previous instructors and to which the children are anesthetized by now. Entrap them first in fascination. Entrap them in a sense of merriment and hopeful expectations. Entrap them in "Bird Gardens."

Even if teachers are obliged to use those scripted

lessons that are commonly believed to be essential instruments of intellectual control for students in the inner-city schools, I still would urge them, if they're given any choice at all, not to start with these materials until they've built a sense of trust and of good-natured camaraderie between the children and themselves. This may require leveling with the kids, even in some rather subtle ways, about the teacher's own opinion of these mandated materials. It may also call for some discussion of the rules and regulations in the school with which the teacher needs the children to comply in order to protect her, and the class, from undue scrutiny.

One of the first things that I told the children in my class was that, if they wanted me to have the freedom to keep on with certain things they seemed to like, they would have to do a really good job in the one specific area I knew was of particular importance to the principal. As you might have guessed, Francesca, this had no connection to the lessons that I taught or, indeed, to anything that took place once I closed the classroom door. It had to do with keeping perfect order when we left the room to file downstairs to the bathrooms or to recess.

The children got the point of this without my needing to explain it further. They already knew what mattered most within the school and proved themselves to be adept at what amounted to a kind of co-conspiracy between us. When we had to go downstairs or file to another room for whatever purpose, they behaved like little soldiers, walking quietly in line, staying on the right side of the stairway, stopping when I told them to, and scarcely whispering a word.

We were soon rewarded by a visit from the principal. "Mr. Kozol," she announced as she stood there in the doorway, "I have a compliment to give your class. The entire school is talking about how these children have been filing in the stairways." She said that this was evidence of how "mature" and "cultured" they'd become. "You can be very proud of them," she said.

One of the children gave me a big "V" for victory the minute that she left the room. For the next six weeks I didn't have a single visit from the principal or anybody else in the administration.

I guess that what I learned from this was that if a teacher knows that he or she is likely to dissent from certain of the pedagogic practices established in a school, the best defense is to be very good at certain *other* practices that matter greatly to the school authorities. If a class that's been unruly for a long, long time suddenly grows calm and well behaved and, superficially at least, obedient to rules that are important to the school, the teacher becomes valuable—and, after a run of teachers who have quit, almost indispensable— because the need to reestablish order in that classroom comes to be the highest possible priority.

I don't want to end this letter on a note that seems unfairly to impugn the motives or priorities of principals in general. In your case, I know you feel that you've been fortunate to have a good insightful principal who shares a number of your views on the prescribed curriculum and who also has a bit of mischief in her personality and seems to enjoy and to appreciate that quality in you.

When I walked into your class last week for the first time, you were sitting in that old black rocking-chair surrounded by your students, who were gathered on the reading rug, some of them with knees scrunched up in front of them, others lying on their stomachs leaning on their elbows. You said that most of them at that point couldn't read or write more than about a dozen words, but you were slowly turning the pages of a word-and-picture book you told me you had loved since you were a child, and you were reading the story to them in that special voice you have which seems to make each sentence sound like something irresistibly delectable. Even the tiny boy, Arturo, whom you referred to as your "little bear," who came into your classroom, as you put it, knowing "almost nothing about anything," was leaning on his elbows looking up at you with a kind of dreamy adoration.

I know how hard you're working with him now to bring him into the big world of letters, sounds, and numbers; but even by that morning, only four weeks after school began, you had already won him over somehow to the very nice idea that he would be surrounded this year by a veil of tenderness and beauty. He obviously felt safe with you and was in the early throes of a child's first love for his teacher.

I saw you give a few quick "looks" to one of your

whisperers and squirmers who was finding it extremely hard to pay attention. But you never let your voice turn cold, and your eyes and those of that restless child met each other in that very candid way that seems to say, "Okay, we understand each other. Now back to the story!"

The children had known you only for a month, but the chemistry had already set in. No curriculum, no rules, no lists of "standards," no externally established regimens, however good or wise they may appear to some, can substitute for this. That bond of trust and tenderness comes first. Without that, everything is merely dutiful—and, generally, deadening. It is not for dutiful aridity that people who love children become teachers.

CHAPTER THREE

Reaching Out to Get to Know the Parents of Our Children

Dear Francesca,

Thank you for inviting me to come and visit with your class on Halloween. It was fun, and I was glad to meet the parents of so many of your children.

And, in answer to your question: No! I don't think you were being unfair in the least in saying that too little help is given to young teachers, before they begin to teach, in thinking about ways in which to build a good relationship with parents. It's one of the most important challenges a teacher faces, and I think this is particularly so when racial issues are at stake within a school, for instance where most of the faculty is white but almost all the children are black or Hispanic. I also agree that it's even more important to reach out with special care to parents who may seem at first to have the least involvement in, or least sustained commitment to, the education of their children.

Obviously, there will always be some parents who, for complicated reasons of their own, may not be responsive even to the best attempts a teacher makes in this regard. Still, I think it's all too easy for young teachers, even quite unconsciously, to write off the parents who are not cooperative at first, instead of trying to discover why it is that some of them will not respond to messages that we send home or seem reluctant to show up for meetings that we schedule. One of the most common statements that I hear from first-year teachers is that parents of the children with the greatest problems are the ones who never seem to make it to class meetings, or to schoolwide meetings, or to individual appointments to which we invite them to discuss the challenges their children face. "She never shows up" or "shows up late" or "seems uncomfortable and edgy." Principals sometimes also note that these are the same parents who do not support the PTA or volunteer to help out with a school trip or a "Pumpkin Fair" or other school activities.

The parents who are most reliable, and most cooperative, those whom the media refer to as "the savvy parents," quickly win the loyalty of teachers because they are genuinely helpful. They also tend to share more of the social styles and the value systems of the teachers, so that teachers feel a natural rapport with them and find it easy to converse with them. In the case of less cooperative parents, on the other hand, I've known many teachers who throw up their hands and, out of sheer impatience or a feeling of futility, give up on any serious attempts to engage their interest and end up never really knowing them.

I always wish I could encourage teachers in these situations to reflect a little on the reasons why some of these parents are resistant to participating in a school's activities and why, when they try to do so, many seem uneasy, even vaguely hostile, and reluctant to speak candidly to teachers. When I was a teacher in Roxbury, it soon became apparent that a number of such parents, who had been given a rockbottom education in some of the same schools 15 or 20 years before, looked upon these schools as places of remembered misery and failure and prolonged years of humiliation. So, even at the age of 28 or 35, they were still uncomfortable in coming to a school and were also insecure about their capability for speaking cogently to teachers about literacy skills, for instance, which in many cases they themselves did not possess.

These were the parents, for example, who did not speak standard English fluently, who typically used double negatives, and verbs like "axed" instead of "asked," a common mispronunciation in some inner-city neighborhoods. They were aware that this was viewed as "ghetto talk" by principals and teachers, with the consequence that they were viewed with subtle disrespect, or feared that they would be so viewed, by middle-class administrators. They didn't want to be subjected to embarrassment and therefore spoke as little as they could at classroom meetings and gave terse responses to the questions they were asked, which was interpreted as evidence of lack of dedication to their children.

Some of these parents had good reasons to distrust their children's principals, who were not always open with them about serious problems in a school and often spoke to them in pedagogic jargon that was not informative but functioned as a barrier to real communication, a pattern that some principals, unhappily, continue to this day. Only a few years ago in the South Bronx, for instance, the principal of P.S. 65, a school I've visited off and on for more than a decade because I've known many children who were students there, refused to level with the parents when the school was facing a high turnover of teachers, which had done tremendous damage to the academic progress of some of the classes at the school.

One of the children I knew well, a charming little girl whose nickname was Pineapple, had no less than seven different teachers in two years. This was not as bad as what my students underwent in Roxbury, but it dealt a heavy blow to Pineapple's basic skills in math and reading and would leave her thoroughly demoralized about her own abilities for several years, despite the fact that she was obviously very bright and was an eager and ambitious student.

Three years later, her younger sister, Angelina, whom I'd known since she was four, was in a fifth grade class whose teacher quit one morning without warning—as it happened, on a day when I was visiting. The principal couldn't find another teacher for the class, so the children were assigned to younger grades in which they were given little more than "busy work" for several weeks. The parents, who, by sheer coincidence, had to come to school that morning to receive report cards, which were given to them by the principal, were not told their children's teacher had walked out. And the principal tried to make sure that I wouldn't learn about this either, by not allowing me to visit Angelina's class, even when I so requested, and by not explaining to me that, if I insisted upon going to her room, I would find no children and no teacher there. She knew that Angelina's parents were close friends of mine and was concerned that I'd relay this information to them, which I surely would have done, in order to enable them to take whatever action still was possible on her behalf.

Good principals are candid with the parents of their students; but there are others who put up a wall of distance and denial that creates an atmosphere of cynicism and distrust among the people in the neighborhood. So even while administrators may deplore that parents of the kids in greatest trouble never show up for school meetings, many of them manage to make sure that those who do show up learn virtually nothing that can help them to defend their children's interests.

At my school in Roxbury, the principal repeatedly complained that parent meetings she announced would be attended typically by only a few dozen parents at the most, and she made unkind remarks about the "culturally deficient values of the Negro parents" who, she said, unlike the previous generation of white parents at the school, were "not committed to their children's education." But the meetings that she held were stiff, perfunctory affairs, never very friendly and not terribly informative. Despite the cupcakes and the cookies that were set out for the parents in a show of hospitality, she seemed to find it hard to loosen up enough to make the parents feel that they were really welcome in the building. If she had a capability for warmth or humor, it was well concealed. The parents who did come to these meetings tried their best to be polite, would nibble at the cookies and attempt to smile in reaction to the frozen smile that the principal displayed.

At first, as a new teacher, I accepted the opinion, widely stated in the school, that the parents were to blame for all of this somehow—although, in retrospect, I can't imagine how. It was one of the very few black women on the faculty who suggested to me that the parents were intimidated by the principal and that the school appeared to them as something like a fortress to which they were given entrance only in submissive roles that made them feel like mute observers and discouraged them from coming back a second time.

My own students, as I've noted, had a dozen substitute teachers prior to the time I was assigned to them. So it didn't seem surprising to me that not many of their parents thought it worth their while to come up to class and talk with me. How long, after all, could they expect that I'd be there? On an impulse, finally, I started visiting the parents of my children after school, driving to their homes in the late afternoons or early evenings and just knocking on their doors.

Some of the parents would look alarmed to see me at their door and would think their child had done something wrong. (Home visits were generally made only by attendance officers or social workers when a child had been truant or had badly misbehaved.) When I explained that I was simply in the neighborhood and wanted to stop by and meet them, I was almost always asked to come inside and was usually asked to stay and visit for a while. If it was near suppertime, parents would often ask if I'd had dinner yet and, if I said I hadn't, would insist that I sit down and have something to eat with them. Sometimes, too, I brought my girlfriend with me, which turned out to make things more relaxed and natural.

I got the impression that the parents liked this opportunity to show us hospitality. And meeting on their own turf, rather than within the school, seemed to free them from the shyness or anxiety they otherwise might feel. I got to know a lot about my students in these visits, but they also helped me to break down the incorrect assumptions I'd imbibed during my college years from reading some authoritative-sounding works of sociology about the parents of black children.

I soon discovered, for example, that not all the

children's homes were "bare of books," as sociologists I'd read had either stated or implied. And even parents who were only marginally literate were familiar often with at least some passages of writing that had special meaning or historical significance for people in the African-American community. One of the parents who insisted that I "sit down right there at that table" and let her prepare me something good to eat introduced me for the first time to the name of Langston Hughes, of whom, like all the other authors of the Harlem Renaissance, I'd never heard at Harvard even though I was a literature major—a reflection, possibly, of yet another kind of "deprivation" than the version urban sociologists tended to emphasize.

I later told my principal about these visits, thinking she'd be pleased with me because one of the catch-cries of that era in the Boston schools was "to bring the school and neighborhood closer together." Instead, however, she expressed dissatisfaction and she told me I had made a bad mistake, which was not in keeping with "appropriate professional behavior," by making visits to my students' homes. "Parents will not respect you if they see you in that way," she said. When I asked her what she meant by "that way," she explained, "In an unprotected social situation."

"Let the parents come up to *you*" (our school was at the top of a hill)—"don't you go down to *them*." She said I'd lose professional respect if I permitted them to know me on a social basis in their homes, or in a store, or on the street. She also said it was especially unwise to bring my girlfriend with me. "You never know," she cautioned me, "what somebody might think. . . ."

This was the first time I had heard the term "professional behavior" used to indicate the opposite of natural behavior. It puzzled me then, and it still does. I didn't believe I'd forfeited my dignity by making friendships with some of my students' families. Much to the reverse, I found it led to long-awaited breakthroughs with some of the students in my room and, best of all, that parents who had not come up to school before now did so, if not frequently, at least on some occasions.

Novice teachers often tell me they've been cautioned, in the same way I was, to be wary of the neighborhoods in which they teach. Physical dangers are evoked most often, but I suspect the physical risks of visiting our students' homes or walking in the streets in which they play are less significant than something more akin to an emotional uneasiness about the act of crossing lines between two worlds of race and social standing. I also think that crossing lines like these as often and as comfortably as we can will teach us more than any of those classes offered frequently to education students about "multicultural relationships," as useful as some of those classes are.

If we only care about establishing relationships with confident and better-educated parents, we need never leave our citadels. But if we want to get beyond that circle of the marginally middle class and reach out to parents who are less empowered and less trustful of us at the start, and on a basis that is *not* perfunctory and psychologically unequal, I don't think we should accept the definition of "professional behavior" as my principal interpreted the term and as it is still conveyed to many first-year teachers.

If our goal as teachers is to serve our children in the best ways that we can, and if it helps us in this effort to learn something of their parents and the lives they lead at home, I don't think we ought to worry whether parents may consider us less worthy of respect when they discover that we lead real lives, and eat real meals, and even maybe like to spend our free time with our girlfriend or our boyfriend. Psychologically healthy people are not likely to be damaged by permitting parents to discover their humanity.

I noticed in your class on Halloween that almost every child's mother, and a good number of fathers too, were in that room. When the children sang the "Pumpkin Song" they had rehearsed with you and suddenly went blank and, for a moment, couldn't come up with a single word, I noticed that the parents looked protectively at *you,* as if they didn't want you to be disappointed.

At the end of the party, you got lots of hugs, not only from the little ones. Your eyes were glowing. You looked so happy and so much at ease among the mothers who were chatting with you by the blackboard while the children, in their pumpkin costumes, got their coats and backpacks from the closet and lined up beside the door.

I know you'd made a few home-visits by that time and that you had given out your cell phone number to the parents and that some of them would call you when they had a question about homework or their child's class behavior. But I could also tell that many of the parents had begun to feel affectionate to you, as if you were a friend to them already.

I wish that students from a school of education could have been there in that room. They would have gotten a wonderful sense of what it's like when somebody who's not afraid to open up her private world a tiny bit, and doesn't feel she has to tighten up her personality to gain respect, is given the reward of loyalty and trust by those whom *she* has trusted with the knowledge of the human being she really is.

CHAPTER FOUR

Teaching the Young, but Learning from the Old

A Cautionary Letter

Dear Francesca,

You've asked me several times what helped me most in getting through that difficult first year in Roxbury. It's not an easy question, because I have never been quite sure of what it was that gave me the stamina to keep on in that classroom, which was commonly referred to, at the time when I was transferred there, as "the worst class in the building" and whose students were described to me by one of the tougher teachers at the school as "simply a rotten group of kids."

I suspect one of the answers, as you probably surmised from my last letter, is the friendship I was able to establish with a number of the parents. But, in strictly pedagogic terms, the greatest help came from an older teacher, not a whole lot older, but a woman who'd been working at the school for six or seven

33

years and, apart from her real gifts as an instructor, had already learned to navigate the complicated politics within the building.

She was a special education teacher, one of the best I've ever had a chance to watch close-up in interaction with her pupils, and had been assigned the students, mostly boys, who were working at the lowest levels. Many of them had neurological or psychiatric disabilities, but others were children who had nothing wrong with them, in clinical respects, but who had disrupted other classes and whom other teachers couldn't bring under control.

Fortunately, she was in the classroom next to mine and had grown acquainted with the children in my class throughout the months before I was assigned to them. She knew what they'd been going through and was therefore able to advise me on the problems of specific children and the academic status of the class in general. If it were not for the multitude of good suggestions she kept passing on to me from day to day, and the personal encouragement she gave me at the ends of days when almost everything seemed to go wrong, I'm not certain I'd have had the courage to remain within that room.

Some of the young teachers whom I've known at P.S. 30, which for many years was one of the better elementary schools in the South Bronx, have told me how much they relied upon the same kind of support from a number of the older teachers in the building. One of those older teachers was my close friend Louis

Bedrock, who had been working at the school for more than 15 years. Another was an African-American woman, Frances Dukes, in whose second grade class I loved to visit because of the masterful but never overbearing way she guided children who had learning problems, or restless children who were easily distracted, back into the strong, demanding rhythms of the schoolday she had charted out for them. A magnificent teacher, who flooded her room with children's books, every one of which she told me she had read and treasured through the years, she had a quiet but commanding look of earned authority within her eyes.

When children misbehaved, she never seemed to need to speak an angry word but stood right there in front of them, folded her arms, and looked directly at them, as their grandmothers might do. The younger teachers loved her and turned to her for comfort and support. Some of them came to think of her as if she were *their* mother or grandmother.

I was in her classroom on the last day of the year before she left the school and went into retirement. Strict as she tried to be, she couldn't keep from crying as the children came up shyly to her desk and handed her the letters they had written her and which, as children often do, some had folded over nearly half a dozen times into tiny packages the size of postage stamps, before she said goodbye to them forever.

This memory of Frances Dukes comes back to me because I think that many first-year teachers miss the opportunity to take advantage of the years of rich experience and of accumulated wisdom about children that the most effective older teachers can convey to them. In their conversations with me, some of these young people give me the impression that they look upon the veteran teachers in their schools as unsophisticated or not "innovative" in whatever way that term is being used, depending on the package of most recent innovations that may happen to be held in favor in a given period of years. I'm sure I was guilty of that error many times, even when I later taught in a much better school, with a larger number of extremely good and seasoned teachers, than the one in which I started out in Roxbury.

You once told me of a problem like this that developed in the year when you were student-teaching at a school in Philadelphia, although at the start, if I remember this correctly, you did not perceive it as a problem, as I know you do today. You described a cluster of young teachers in the building who attached themselves to one another, spoke of their frustrations and their insecurities with one another, worked on lessons with each other, and, because they shared so many of your tastes and values and had come from backgrounds not unlike your own, became your closest friends within the school—all of which sounds natural and, on the face of it, seems to make perfect sense.

Unwittingly, however, as you later recognized, the camaraderie that you established with these other teachers of your age had the effect of leading you to pretty much ignore the older teachers in the building, those who had been working there for decades in some cases and who would remain there after most of the young teachers you'd befriended had moved on to other schools or districts or, as you have told me, gave up teaching altogether.

This is the part that you have said now makes you "squirm" when you think back upon the consequences that this had: Most of the older teachers in the school were African-American. All of the young women who became your friends happened to be white. Without so intending, you'd been drawn into a situation that was bound to polarize the faculty between the young newcomers and the relatively "set" and staid and perhaps not always terribly exciting veterans, whom some of your friends appeared to view as obstacles to "new ideas," much as bright teenagers often have an unkind tendency to dismiss or denigrate the values or opinions of their parents.

This may have been an accurate perception in some cases. Every ethnic group, it seems, turns out its share of stick-in-the-mud warhorses who refuse to reexamine any of their practices, no matter what may change within the world or in the neighborhood around them. Still, as you have noted since, there were also plenty of terrific older teachers in that school with whom it would have been to your advantage to establish close relationships. And, as you now recognize, the cliquishness of that small group of relatively privileged young women to whom you'd attached yourself inevitably left those older teachers with the sense that they were being viewed with disrespect or generational hostility. Add to this the racial factor, and the end result, as you've observed, was a kind of covert sense of warfare between young and old, and white and black, within the precincts of one building.

Some of the young white teachers I have met, several of whom came into public education through one of the "fast-track" programs to which I've referred, have found themselves in situations not unlike the one that you described. A number of them, unhappily, have subsequently left the public schools and gravitated into semi-private charter schools, or joined with others of their age to create a new school of their own, in which they give me the impression that they feel relieved at being liberated from the "oldtime" faculty and principals with whom they worked before. More than a few of them, I'm sad to say, are now supporting privatizing schemes.

In your case, Francesca, it was clear that you would never turn in that direction. The entire process by which you began to reexamine your experience in that first year in Philadelphia and your persistence in believing that, no matter what frustrations you had undergone, the ultimate struggle for the education of our children will, and must, take place within the borders of the public schools themselves, is one of those redemptive stories that we seldom hear about in media reports. The media more often celebrate those whiz-kid graduates of colleges like Yale and Princeton who abandon public schools in order, as the privatizing forces claim, to "break the mold" of education by creating what, admittedly, are sometimes quite impressive schools but, in the larger scheme of things, are little less than boutique institutions.

After my first year in Boston, I regret to say that, for a year or two, I also grew intrigued by these appealing possibilities. Looking back upon my state of mind during that period, I recognize an element not just of natural impatience, even healthy indignation, at the terrible conditions I'd encountered at the school in which I'd worked, but also of a brisk, smart-aleck certitude that within a mere ten months I'd somehow learned enough to turn my back upon the efforts of those tens of thousands of good teachers elsewhere in my city and throughout the nation who remained within the trenches of the public schools that served the vast majority of children.

Some good advice from wiser and much older friends brought me to reconsider the direction I was heading. Instead, I sought and found another teaching job at an elementary school in which the principal was empathetic with at least some of the practices I was attracted to. And even though she frequently would sit me down to counsel me on errors I was making—I had a hard time learning to teach math effectively at first, one of several areas in which my inexperience was evident—she did this in a manner that was not censorious and was almost always helpful.

39

This was in a suburban school that had recently become part of an interdistrict integration program that enabled inner-city children, on a voluntary basis, to enroll in some of the top-rated systems just outside of Boston. So I had the opportunity for the first time to see black children who had started out in several of the city's bleakest and most deeply segregated schools enrolled in classes in a pleasant-looking and uncrowded building—I now had 19 students in my class, instead of 35—where virtually all of them made far more rapid progress than they'd ever made before. The parents of the kids from Roxbury seemed to feel at ease when they made visits to the school, because the principal was effortlessly open and relaxed with them, and she was sincerely grateful that they trusted her to educate their children.

She could be strict with teachers when she had to be, but she was also an engagingly good-natured person, a romantic soul at heart who seemed to look on life and childhood and education as a limitless adventure. She liked to shock me and the other teachers by telling us of what she called her "youthful indiscretions" when she was an Army nurse in World War II in Italy, although she never spelled out what those "indiscretions" were, which made them sound more wicked and exciting.

One day, when the children in my class were working on their book reports while listening to music from a tape of operatic tunes I had brought to school, the principal waltzed into the room, grabbed me around the waist, and made me dance with her in front of all my students. I was embarrassed because I'm an awful dancer, but my students thoroughly enjoyed this spectacle and, inevitably, teased me later without mercy by their imitations of my awkwardness. My earlier impressions of administrative cheerlessness in public education dissipated quickly.

You were wise enough not to permit yourself the detour I had briefly taken. I recall your telling me that, when you started looking for a teaching job in Boston, you purposely avoided looking at the charter schools but searched for a position in an ordinary public school and found one before long in which the principal appeared to have a nice relationship with parents and a good rapport with children and where she also made it clear, as did several of the older teachers, that you would be welcome on their faculty.

I know you feel you made the right decision. When you told me just before Thanksgiving that your principal had started phoning you at night after you had told her that you'd grown discouraged by the reading difficulties of a number of the children, I remember your relief and the restorative effect this had upon your state of mind. Your voice was full of its old energy again. I also remember the encouragement you felt when one of the fifth grade teachers, who had had far more experience than you, started coming down into your classroom in the afternoons and sharing with you challenges that she was facing too.

In one of his best-known poems, W. H. Auden

wrote of Dr. Sigmund Freud, "All that he did was to remember like the old and be honest like children." A first-year teacher who is only 22 or 23 years old obviously cannot "remember like the old," but he or she *can* learn not only about teaching practices but, often more important, about moral steadiness and personal self-confidence from those who *do* remember.

I know that Auden's poetry or, as you have put it, "poetry of almost any kind at all"—even poetry of temperament and teaching style—does not tend to be included in those "methods and materials of teaching" courses or those "educational foundations" courses that are standard elements of teacher preparation. And even when they are, the poetry of teaching gets obliterated all too quickly by the pressure that school systems feel to buckle under to the mandates coming from state boards of education and, increasingly, from Washington. To "be honest like children" is not part of any state curriculum for teachers I have ever seen. "To remember like the old" may well sound even quaint and rather useless in an age when lists of "scientifically" established "things that work" dominate the discourse of the pedagogic think tanks and appear to make the learnings of our elders sound irrelevant.

I guess it's not surprising that so many older teachers, partly for this reason—and I'm thinking of some teachers who can still turn up the voltage in the classroom when they want and who also tell me how much they will miss the sense of expectation that each morning holds for them at school—go into retirement much sooner than they need to. They seem to get the message that they are regarded as expendable.

Then, too, politicians in some states and school officials in some districts seem only too eager to persuade their older teachers to retire early. If these veteran teachers, who are working at the higher salaries which their seniority commands, can be replaced by novice teachers who, of course, work at much lower scales of pay, officials can save money for their state or district.

Some of these older teachers, certainly—I'm thinking of a few who were real terrors at my school in Roxbury—are anything but sources of encouragement and wisdom and *ought* to be replaced as rapidly as possible. But the best among them bring a sense of personal stability and of assimilated selflessness into a faculty, as well as all the nuts and bolts of classroom management and of the good instructional approaches they've acquired. Many also can help first-year teachers in developing relationships with parents in the neighborhood. Sometimes they've known three generations of the families who've passed through the school and can enrich young teachers with an understanding of the history of lived experience in the communities they serve.

Political leaders who "remember like the old" are, unfortunately, all too scarce these days. "To be honest like children" is a rarity in politics as well. The younger teachers in any state or district where attempts are being made to pressure veteran teachers to retire sooner than they need to will, I hope, have the good sense to raise their voices to defend the interests of the old. If not, it is they, I am convinced, as well as the children whom they teach, who will in the long run suffer most.

CHAPTER FIVE

Wild Flowers

Dear Francesca,

I'm glad you liked the quote I sent you from Fred Rogers. He often made the same point about listening more carefully to children than we usually do. "At quiet times," he told me once, "young children give us glimpses of some things that are eternal."

As you've noticed, they are also frequently inclined to give us glimpses of pure silliness, as well as of the many clever strategies that they devise for handling the minor challenges they face, like getting us to do a certain thing for them they have decided we should do. They are also very fond, in my experience at least, of telling us their secrets.

"This is a secret between you and me," a little girl named Ariel told me at her school in the South Bronx one day when she was eight years old. "My

45

nickname is Potato, but my mother says I'm beautiful and calls me Wild Flower."

"It's a beautiful name," I said.

"I think so too," said Ariel. "I don't *like* it when the other kids call me Potato. . . ."

When I asked her, nearly two years later, for permission to repeat this, she said, "Oh my God! I can't *believe* I told you that!"

A friend of mine who came with me to visit in the Bronx said that Ariel reminded her of one of those "oval-faced madonnas by Murillo" in the Prado in Madrid. Her teachers spoke of her natural refinement and her kindness to the younger children and respect for older people. She used to like to whisper secrets in my ear when her teachers let me help her with her reading, and she liked to hand me little notes and would make me promise that I wouldn't tell these things to anybody else.

Some children who reveal their secrets to us in these hesitant and bashful ways seem to feel empowered later to reveal themselves in more outgoing ways as they begin to gain the literary skills to write in classroom journals or to make their first attempts at writing poetry. Ariel started writing poetry when she was in fourth grade. One of the first poems she wrote was a tender effort to remember her grandfather and was called "The Soothing Hand."

In couplets that were written in the rhythms of a normal conversation, she compared the love she felt for her deceased grandfather to "a bird without grief" that was "soaring through the underworld" and "spreading peace." She said she loved him even though she never knew him, because he had died before she had been born. She said she knew that he was "powerful" but also "very gentle"—"not a man of fighting." She was sure that he was watching over her in heaven.

Ariel went to P.S. 30, where the atmosphere was more informal, and the principal more flexible, than at Pineapple's school. Her teacher left a lot of time for children to do independent writing that was unrelated to the school's curriculum, not the kind of writing that derives from "prompts" but writing that derived from memories they'd shared with him or personal reflections they had mentioned in their journals. He later showed me poems that other children in the class were writing. All of them were not as solemn as the one that Ariel had written to remember her grandfather. One of the smallest children in the class, a precocious boy named Reginald who wore thick glasses which he was always breaking or misplacing, wrote this little poem in prose about his mom and dad: "If your mom says 'I love you' and your dad says 'I love you,' you have to say 'I love you too.'" If you don't, he said, "that would be rude" and "they might send you to your room without your supper."

"Little animals in your house, acting like they own it," wrote a boy named Santiago about mice or other unknown creatures he could hear behind the wall. "Babyes cry for food and love. At night: dangers in the dark."

The teacher's door was covered with the students' writings, even those that were less polished or not spelled correctly or where sentences were incomplete or ran on into one another. I know he made the children go through several drafts of poems or stories that they showed him; but, after they had done their best, I'm glad he put their writings on display even with the errors that had not yet been corrected.

When I taught in Boston and then in the more relaxed and less constrictive school out in the suburbs I've described, I used to do the same thing, putting up the still-imperfect writings of my students with all the cross-outs and erasures and misspellings and the words they seemed to like to capitalize for no good reason other than the fact that certain words seemed to possess a special power for them and, in their opinion, merited unusual attention. It's not hard to teach a child how to fix these things, to clean up spelling errors and to save their capital letters for the starts of sentences and names of places and people later on. Getting the good stuff down on paper as the children write it, with its freshness and its vigor still intact, was, for me, always the first priority.

Many teachers are discouraged from displaying less-than-perfect writings by their students in the inner-city schools I visit nowadays. In Pineapple's school, supervisors used to come by with a clipboard to examine wall displays. Teachers were given a list of no more and no less than "five essential elements" of a successful wall display. Imperfect spelling, crossed-out words, even erasures, were considered serious infractions.

It came to the point where one of the best young teachers at the school told me she was ordered to correct such errors in her own handwriting or by typing the entire piece correctly before she could put it on the wall. When she told her principal that she refused to doctor writings by her students, she was warned that there would be "a letter" in her file that would indicate her noncompliance.

Most principals, thank God, are not so tyrannical as this. Very few, I think, would ask their teachers to engage in such unethical behavior. But the reluctance to allow a child's words to be displayed with imperfections, as the child actually wrote them, is increasingly familiar. System-wide consistency in presentation of a child's "product" (one of a number of such terms imported into inner-city education from the business world) tends to prohibit the display of those endearing, sometimes very charming, also sometimes very funny errors that are seen on bulletin boards in good suburban schools where these draconian demands have not yet taken hold.

I'd like to go back to Mr. Rogers' observation about listening more carefully to children's words. One of the reasons why this has become more difficult in recent years is the insistence of most urban systems that, at almost any given moment of the day, teachers need to be "on task" (another term that comes from the industrial arena) and that the only task that matters is the one that's stipulated by an "outcome" or "objective" that's been posted on the wall.

Setting up objectives for the lessons that we teach is obviously an old and honored practice. I don't want to leave you with the incorrect impression that I question this. The problem in too many schools is not in the idea of an objective in itself but in the fierce relentlessness with which pursuit of that objective is enforced and in the disturbing fact that teachers seldom get to choose their own objectives since these are, in large part, dictated by the state.

The overdetermined lesson plans now commonly in use in inner-city neighborhoods, which are often written word for word from scripted programs that are handed to the teacher and intended to keep children on an absolutely straight line to the destination of the next high-stakes exam, leave little time for teachers to pay close attention to those children who won't give the answers we are told we must elicit from them or who, even more unpardonably, ignore our pre-planned questions and insist on asking better questions of their own.

These minute-by-minute lesson plans remind me of those miserable 16-city European tours where people are told that they can never leave the bus to wander down a street that looks intriguing to them, or sit down and have a drink at a sidewalk restaurant that isn't listed on the schedule for the tour, because such deviations and indulgences may cause us to arrive too late at the next stopping-point. People who insist on climbing off that bus too many times are soon regarded as unwelcome passengers. The same is true of children who will not confine themselves to the itinerary that the lesson plans demand.

In a class discussion, for example, if a child interrupts to say something that's not responsive to the purpose of the lesson—something that may matter to him deeply, something that he just finds funny, something that has moved him so much that he has to struggle not to cry—the teacher in these rigid situations is reluctant to allow him to go on with his idea and often feels obliged to cut him off or even to admonish him with some abruptness.

A second grade teacher told me once that six-year-olds and seven-year-olds are "gifted artists" at subverting lesson plans. One of the likable tendencies of children of that age is to meander off into the blissful kingdom of irrelevance as frequently as possible. "Teacher?" the child says. "Guess what?" "What?" the teacher says. "I went to the zoo on Sunday with my Uncle Pookey—and guess what?" "What?" the teacher says again. "I saw a baby bear!" And then the child starts to pile on the "ands" and "buts" for one of those seemingly eternal run-on sentences that cheerfully forgets where it began. But sometimes at the end of all those "ands" and "buts" there's a piece of hidden treasure where the child tells us something that we never knew about him up to now. And good teachers *use* that piece of hidden treasure as a key to unlock motivation and to bring the child back into the classroom work that must be done, but with a sense of purpose now that would have been absent, and remained invisible to her, if she had been forced to cut him off.

"Okay, sweetie, that's a beautiful story that you told us. Now let's see if, when we go back to our desks, you can write it down for me with all those interesting details you included. . . ."

I've seen you do this, for example, with Shaniqua, letting her wander off and have her moment in the sun and letting the other children tell her what they liked the best about her story if they want, then shepherding her gently back into the work of spelling all those words she's used and putting them into something that resembles sentences.

Once a child writes down something that she actually cares about, it's easy enough to go back through it with her, word by word, to show her things that she left out. (Young children, as I notice almost every time a teacher lets me work with students in a first or second grade, often seem to hear a word they thought they wrote and they even *read* the word aloud to us, as if it's there, and are surprised when we point out to them that they forgot to write it down.) Then, too, once there's something of real substance on the page, it's not hard to help our students see where stopping-points should come and where new sentences ought to begin because they *make* these stops and starts themselves when they are reading to us.

In many over-driven classrooms, children never

get a chance to put that substance on the page to start with or, even if they do, they tend to lose the freshness of their words because so many teachers have been trained to try to "upgrade" words their students use by suggesting "better words" they ought to use, especially in schools that serve those children who, because of where they live, are labeled "culturally deprived."

This is a long-standing problem, I'm afraid. When I taught in Boston, for example, a writing specialist came into my class one day to demonstrate a lesson. She asked the children for an antonym for "fat" (antonyms and homonyms and synonyms were part of the curriculum in fourth grade at my school), and one of my students, a girl named Alabama, perked right up and gave her "skinny" in response.

The writing expert furrowed her brow and left an expectant pause. Then, with a smile that she'd obviously practiced through the years, she said to the child, "Let's put on our thinking cap and see if we can't find a *nicer* word than 'skinny'" and she soon induced the child to say "slender" in its place.

I understood the reason why the writing teacher did this. She was a self-confident and determined person who sincerely felt that she was doing something beneficial for a child of this neighborhood by imposing a more proper-sounding word upon the child's style of speech. But even though I didn't dare to say this, because I knew it would hurt the writing teacher's feelings, I thought "skinny" was a better word, a livelier and far more pungent word, than "slender." The writing teacher's word might fit into the genteel social pages of newspapers or the text of fashion magazines, but "skinny" was a word that children actually use and, to be honest, one that I'd more likely choose as well. It occurred to me that if that child ever got to college, a good writing teacher with an ear for the vitality of words might try his hardest to get "skinny" back again.

Earlier in the year, the writing teacher posted on the wall a list of what she called "ten-dollar adjectives" that children were supposed to use in writing book reports. "Humorous" and "interesting" and "colorful" and "adventurous" are four that I wrote down and still recall. Words like "boring," "neat," "terrific," "scary," "funny," "sad," "pathetic," "deadly dull," or "idiotic" weren't included. I remember wondering how often any child, black or white, or rich or poor, would describe a book she'd read as "colorful" or "humorous" in normal conversation.

Similar practices, and others even more devitalizing, are familiar in some of the urban schools I visit now. In one fifth grade class I visited a year ago, for instance, children were presented with a list of 44 "official sentences," which I was told had come from a state document, that they were supposed to use in speaking of their levels of ability. "I am proficient," according to one of these sentences, which was posted on the wall above the children's heads, "in considering the six traits of effective writing so I can improve my work before I share it with my partner."

The notion that there really are "six traits," no more, no less, of "effective writing" did not sound convincing to me. Most writers, I suspect, would tell us this is utter nonsense. It was apparently something that somebody in the state bureaucracy had taken without thinking very much from a text he might have read on ways of teaching children about sentence structure. But it was the presence of the word "proficient" in this sentence ("I am proficient in considering . . .") that seemed the most bewildering to me. Why would a child in the fifth grade ever want or need to learn a word so utterly unnatural? This kind of language does not bring high culture to the children of the poor; it brings, at best, the mediocre culture of officials who somehow believe that taking a good solid Anglo-Saxon noun like "skill" and tacking on three extra syllables to turn it into a "proficiency" is evidence of intellectual sophistication. Words like this do not teach literacy skills; they teach pomposity.

If the ultimate goal in all of this is to introduce our students to the use of words of several syllables, there are plenty of big and interesting words children are attracted to more readily than the ones imposed upon them by the kind of poster that I noticed in that room. One child in the Bronx I've known for many years, whose name is Sierra Smiley, took a liking to the word "persnickety" when she was in third grade. She had heard her grandma use the word. She liked the sound of it. She didn't spell it right the first time, but her teacher helped her work it out phonetically.

I think the reason why she liked the word is that it sounds like what it means. The syllables crackle like the voice of someone who might be a little crotchety and sound a trifle fussy if her grandchildren annoyed her. If a teacher's goal is to induce her students to use words of many syllables, I should think "persnickety" would advance the cause a whole lot better than a piece of pedagogic deadwood like "proficiency."

I remember your anecdote about one of the children that you taught in Philadelphia who asked you what the word "bamboozle" means. You said you teased her with a hint. "It's something that you're very good at doing to your teachers, and especially to me!" Then you said you made her use the dictionary to find out the definition of the word and how it's spelled. After that, you said she used it every time she had a chance. "Bamboozle" has a pleasant sound. It's hard to say it without smiling.

I guess the message that I wish I could pass on to teachers who are entering the public schools for the first time is to enjoy what children say and not insist on what somebody tells us they're *supposed* to say. Celebrate words like "skinny" and "bamboozle" and "persnickety"! Leave "the six traits of effective writing" and the listings of "proficiencies" to bureaucrats and literacy program planners in departments of curriculum. Don't inflict dead verbiage on living children. And no matter what a school system demands in terms of dreary mandates to remain eternally on task, leave time for the little Ariels and precocious little boys like Reginald who can't remember where they left their glasses to sneak up beside us anytime they want while we're engaged in something else and whisper us their secrets.

CHAPTER SIX

The Little Piper

A Few Reflections on the Kids
Who Make It Clear That They're
Determined Not to Like Us

Dear Francesca,

I've been wrestling with your question about children who come into school with a defiant attitude that seems to challenge every effort that we make to teach them and who seem to mock our very presence in the classroom, as if they've decided in advance that we are someone they won't like and who probably should not be trusted.

As a kind of text for what I want to say, I'd like to try to answer you by starting with an anecdote from one of my favorite authors, Daniel Defoe, who is remembered usually these days as one of the first great novelists of the English language but who also wrote a powerful documentary work, A Journal of the Plague Year, which would probably be classified as journalistic fiction nowadays.

In this book, Defoe tells the famous story of a piper in the streets of London who had fallen sound asleep, perhaps from having had too much to drink, during a time of plague and, having been thought to be a victim of the plague, was carted off by the grave-diggers. "At length," he writes, "the cart came to the place where the bodies were to be thrown into the ground." The piper awakened and, raising his head a little from the cart, he called out, "Hey! Where am I?"

This, says Defoe, frightened the grave-diggers. But after a pause, one of the grave-diggers said, "Lord, bless us! There's somebody . . . not quite dead!" So another person called to him and said, "Who are you?" The piper answered, "I am the poor piper. Where am I?" "Where are you?" said the man. "Why, you are in the dead-cart, and we are going to bury you." "But I ain't dead, though, am I?" said the piper—which, says Defoe, "made them laugh a little."

In New York, at 32nd Street and Herald Square, children from a homeless shelter called the Martinique Hotel used to run out into traffic, armed with rags and buckets, and attempt to wipe the windshields of the cars stopped at the lights. There was a certain gaiety about this. Kids would shout to one another—"Hey! I got two dollars!"—and would sometimes taunt the drivers, who would frequently roll up their windows, leaving just a crack perhaps to slip some money out but to be sure the children couldn't touch them.

The manic leaping and dashing into traffic used to make me worry that the kids would get run down by an impatient driver racing to get past the lights. Some of these drivers were suburbanites or tourists who would not have known there was a dangerous and squalid shelter holding 1,600 children and their mothers right there one block from Fifth Avenue and half-a-block from Macy's. The children, inadvertently perhaps, compelled them to discover something they would rather not have had to know.

Beggar children in Bombay sing a haunting song: "We are the dust beneath your feet. We are the flowers that never bloom." But the wiry little children of the Martinique Hotel refused to be abased to this degree. They shouted their presence, cursed at people who ignored them, and they yelled their victories to one another when a generous person now and then might hand them a five-dollar bill, or even be impelled to ask their name or where they lived or if they had a mother to take care of them.

But even when a stranger tried to treat them with solicitude, there was an insistent sense of mockery about the way the children would react. They seemed to draw their energy out of a deep-seated fury at the marginality to which they'd been consigned. It almost seemed they hated most the people who were kind to them.

I meet many children like the little piper sitting in the classrooms of the public schools I visit in the poorest sections of Los Angeles, Chicago, and New York. These are usually the hardest kids to teach and pose the greatest challenges to teachers. And this is

especially the case with teachers who are just beginning their careers and whose initial insecurity may
function as an invitation to such children to confront
them and to break down their self-confidence right
from the start. Some of these children are so outright
rude, sarcastic, and denunciatory to the teacher, and
so loaded with hostility to other children, that they
single-handedly can bring almost all serious instruction to a halt.

Many young teachers, as compassionate and patient as they try to be, tend to react to kids like these
by making what is basically a surgical decision: "I cannot do a good job for the other children in the room if
I permit this boy to take up so much of my time and
ruin things for everybody else." So, even though it goes
against their principles to do this, they tend to isolate
that child in whatever way they can and try to lock him
out of their attention for extended periods of time.

I noticed, when I visited your class the first time,
that there was a child like this in your room who gave
you so much trouble that you had to put him at a
table in the corner where he could not constantly dis-
tract the other children from their work. I knew that
you felt bad about this because you reluctantly con-
ceded that you thought he was a fascinating child.
You said, "I kind of love him for his style, his defi-
ance, but he has no common sense and absolutely no
politeness."

His tall and loose-limbed body had a gangly and
slightly comical appearance, which I thought that he

exploited like a stage comedian when he was walking through the room. You said, "He acts as if he's made of Silly Putty. He never just sits down like other children do. He makes it a theatrical performance just to get back to his chair." You also told me that the first week of the year, before you put him at the table in the corner, he vaulted over the back of his chair one afternoon and kicked someone behind him in the face.

On the morning I was there, he didn't strike me as malicious to the other children. He had his head down on his table, pressed against his folded arms, and simply seemed to have decided to ignore you and the other students altogether. When I went and stood there near him in his corner and said "Hi" to him, he looked me over briefly and then blew me off without a word. He didn't even bother to lift up his head. He just sized me up from where he was and closed his eyes again.

One of the other kids, however, told me, *"He is mean!"* And there was one week, as I recall—it might have been the week after I visited—when you said you had to ask your principal to keep him in her office for the first part of each day because he kept on getting up and wandering around the room and looking over children's desks and doing irritating things like grabbing their erasers or their pencils.

The only time I saw him acting somewhat less resistant was when he was on the reading rug one day while you were reading from that lovely book about "the grouchy ladybug," one of the many books by Eric

Carle I noticed in your room. He obviously liked the
story and paid good attention for a while, although
even then he kept on pushing other kids who were
taking up the space he seemed to think he needed for
himself so he could stretch out on his belly and lean
on his elbows and look up at you as you were pointing
to the pictures.

As soon as the story was over, however, he re-
verted to his customary manner and, by a circuitous
route which I thought was clearly meant to be annoying to you and the other children, he made his way
back to his table, where he thoroughly turned you off
as if he had a TV clicker and decided that your program wasn't good enough to watch.

The next time I was there, I saw that you had
moved him to a desk beside the blackboard where
you had a better chance to keep an eye on him and
where you could try to bring him in from time to time
to join some of the class activities, a few of which, like
moving around those red and blue and yellow bars of
different lengths, he seemed to find intriguing. You
told me that he finally confessed to you that he had
gotten bored from doing almost nothing all day long
and gave you to understand that he was now prepared to let you make his life more interesting, if you
had the skill to do it, for the hours when he had to be
in class.

In November, when I visited again, he didn't
look so hostile anymore but still would interrupt the
other kids while they were working on their journals,

or were doing independent reading, and he still kept getting into quarrels about pencils, colored crayons, or whatever other objects he could grab from other children's desks and then insist they were his own. When he did this, I was impressed to see you use your sternest-looking frown—you got quite good at that—to get him to stay relatively quiet and polite for periods of time.

You told me that his name was Dobie but that he insisted upon being known as "Captain Black." And I recall that, on an impulse just before Thanksgiving, you made a visit to his home and brought him a box of brownies you had baked for him. You said that you were shocked to find he didn't have a bedroom but was sleeping on a small bed in the same room as his sister and his mom. But you also told me you were heartened by the way that he reacted to your visit. His tendency to mock a friendly gesture and distrust its meaning seemed to have dissolved somewhat by then. You said that you were startled when he told his mother you were "a nice lady," "the best teacher in my school"—how could he possibly say that to his mother when he gave you so much trouble all day long?—and he gave you at least what you said was "a ho-hum hug" when it was time to leave.

In academic terms, the first sign of a break-through I could sense was when he started filling up his spiral pad with bits of narrative that opened up some of those angry memories and fears he'd been reluctant to reveal to you before. You said that you began to use these sentences to introduce him to the very grown-up task of looking at his own words and rewriting them so that the vowels, some of which you said that he already knew but stubbornly ignored, began to go where they belonged. After you had told him that old saying about "silent e," which, when it follows a consonant (I hope I've got this right), makes the vowel that comes just before the consonant into a "long O" or "long A" or "E" or "I" or "U"—I think you said it makes that vowel "brave enough to say its name"—you told me he kept "jumping" you by telling you this rule, as if you'd never heard of it, each time that it applied.

It was only eight weeks earlier that you had thought of recommending him for a "referral," which would probably have led to his assessment as a boy who was "developmentally delayed" or "psychologically impaired," or something worse—one of those many labels that so often end up as the self-fulfilling prophecies that stigmatize a child not just for one year but for the course of his career in public school.

I try to bend over backwards not to start extracting overly big meanings from small spurts of progress since, in doing so, we tend to dwarf and overstate the first few modest steps that previously resistant children suddenly begin to take once the dam that held them back is broken and at least a little stream of curiosity and stirrings of their intellectual vitality begins to flow. Nonetheless, if there's a lesson to be learned from his experience with you, and yours with him—

because relationships like these have always struck me as a kind of complicated and mysterious duet between a teacher and a very vulnerable child—it may be simply this: None of us should make the error of assuming that a child who is hostile to us at the start, or who retreats into a sullenness and silence or sarcastic disregard for everything that's going on around him in the room, does not have the will to learn, and plenty of interesting stuff to teach *us* too, if we are willing to invest the time and the inventiveness to penetrate his seemingly implacable belief that grownups do not mean him well and that, if he trusts us, we will probably betray or disappoint him.

I do not mean, Francesca, in saying what I did about assigning "labels" to a student, that children who have serious psychological problems, or other kinds of problems such as speech pathology or difficulty in the processing of words they hear, cannot benefit tremendously from being given extra help by speech or language specialists, for instance, or by school psychologists. Clinical needs, when they're for real, require clinical solutions. And special education teachers, like the one who taught a number of severely damaged children in the room right next to mine in Boston and who helped me so much at the start, are priceless assets in a school in almost any neighborhood at all.

At the same time, I think that teachers need to be as patient as they can, and rely on every bit of ingenuity that they command, before they assign these kids to categories out of which, as they move from grade to grade, they sometimes never can escape. "It becomes a trap," you said. "It's so much easier for children to go in than to get out." In Dobie's case I think that time has proven that you made the right decision.

When Dobie finally started writing longer, more coherent entries in his spiral pad, and when the floodgates opened up enough so he could vent more of the anguish he had hidden up until that time, you told me you were startled once again to find out how much turbulence and social violence he had already undergone. Turning that pent-up anguish into satisfaction at the progress he was making in his literacy skills may not have saved him from the other sorrows and endangerments he's likely to encounter in the years ahead. Even if the progress he is making now should be sustained during his next four years in elementary school, there are the ever-present risks that he will face when he moves on into the less protective world of middle school. Still, victories are victories. And I recall that when he wrote that powerful piece of narrative for you about the Sunday afternoons on which he visited his father, who was in a prison out in western Massachusetts (I think you said that he's still there) several hours from his home, you said it made you cry. You told me that you put it on your bedroom wall.

It seems that Dobie has accepted you at last and sees you as a special friend. The letter you showed me that he gave you just before the holidays will, I bet, soon earn a place up on your wall as well. "Dear Lady Mamalade," he wrote—you told me he had asked you what you liked for breakfast and you said that you loved orange marmalade and butter on your toast— "I think yur wunder full, plus also cheezy, plus also good and wunder full. Love, Captin Black." I liked especially what he squeezed in down at the bottom of the page: "P.S. And you beter tell me Thank You for this leter be kuz I workt hard on it!"

You said he told you that this was your Christmas present—"the only one" you'd get from him, he added. It's hard to imagine any other present that was likely to have made you happier. If I were Dobie's teacher, I'd be every bit as proud as you were to receive a letter like that from a child who was so determined to dislike you when he walked into your classroom in September.

You told me once you knew that you were fortunate to have a class of only 20 children and one in which there weren't a bunch of other kids who started out distrusting you the way that Dobie did. I know a teacher in New York who had three boys like Dobie in her class last year, and several girls with very hostile attitudes as well. And these were older children— I think they were third graders—and it was a big class, nearly 30 students, so she couldn't give each of these kids the time and the attention that she knew they needed and deserved. She told me that she often cried at night out of frustration.

This is why I think that class size is so terribly

important. In a class of 20 children or, as I saw not long ago in one of the elementary schools not far from Boston, only 16 children in one room, kids who come into the class with an edgy attitude but a lot of pent-up energy, as Dobie did, are far more likely to be given personal attention than are children in the badly overcrowded classes that I visit in so many other inner-city schools. The likable humor that emerged at last in Dobie's personality and the powerful feelings that he finally got down on paper get "locked in" for kids like these. When they're not disrupting class, they sit and brood and look as if they feel encaged. It's like seeing spirit trapped in stone.

Langston Hughes wrote something strong and memorable about the often gifted little rebels who, because of their rebellious ways, are written off too rapidly and ultimately penalized severely by society.

Nobody loves a genius child.
"Kill him—and let his soul run wild!"

Well, all these little rebels who begin by flaunting their distrust and adversarial abilities in front of teachers in the first months of the school-year are not "genius children." But many of these children do have gifts to bring us if we grant ourselves, and if our schools allow us, time enough to listen to them carefully, as Mr. Rogers counseled us, and also time to forge the subtle bond that will permit them to reveal themselves.

I think that Dobie has been blessed to have you as his teacher; but blessings in the very special world of elementary school have always had a lovely reciprocity. I can tell from the elation and the tenderness for Dobie that were so apparent when you phoned me here last night that you feel you have been blessed by knowing him as well. He dared to open up his heart to you. You made that possible.

CHAPTER SEVEN

The Uses of "Diversity"

Dear Francesca,

I thought the presentation that you made during the conference in Vermont about "diversity" last week was pretty damn amazing. I was glad you had a chance to speak. Too many of those education conferences never give real teachers any opportunity to voice their own beliefs.

I also agree with you entirely that the way the subject of diversity is introduced to children in most public schools has come to be a very bland and boring ritual in which the word itself, "diversity," has been adulterated to the point where it can only mock reality instead of openly describing it.

"The ugly little secret," as you put it, is that there is almost no diversity at all in most of the schools in which diversity curricula are generally used. The word, you said, has come to be a cover-up for situations to which it can't possibly apply.

As you've noticed, this is right in keeping with the way the word is used in education journals and the media. There is a seemingly agreed-upon convention, in the written press especially, never to use a plain, unvarnished term like "racial segregation"—not, at least, in reference to the city where the newspaper is published—if there's any way the term can be avoided. This is the case even in a narrative description of a segregated school, where journalists have learned to do semantic somersaults in order not to use a word that may do injury to civic pride. High schools that enroll as few as six or seven white or Asian students in a total population of as many as 3,000, and where every other child in the building is black or Hispanic, are commonly referred to, in the parlance of reporters, as "diverse."

School systems employ this euphemism too. In a school I visited last fall in Kansas City, for example, I was provided with a document that said the school's curriculum "addresses the needs of children from diverse backgrounds." But as I went from class to class I didn't see a single child who was white or Asian—or Hispanic, for that matter. The principal, when I pressed her on the demographics of the school, said that 99.6 percent of students there were black.

In a similar document, the school board of a district in New York referred to "the diversity" and "rich variations" in the "ethnic backgrounds" of its student population. But when I looked at the racial numbers that the district had provided to the state, I learned that there were 2,800 black and Hispanic children in the system, one Asian child, and three whites. If school boards cannot bring themselves to call things by their right names, it's not surprising that the same misleading use of language infiltrates instructional materials as well.

The pattern carries through to many of those so-called "civil rights" curricula which tend to function, as you said, not as challenges to critical analysis of present-day realities, and even less as provocations to take action on those challenges, but instead, to use your words, as "soporific pacifiers" that provide a feel-good resolution to the contradictions school officials do not dare to name.

Many deeply segregated public schools pay tribute, for example, to the history of civil rights by introducing children to a set of lesson plans about the struggles of the past while steering clear of any reference to the struggles of a comparable order that remain before their generation now. Typically, these lesson plans rely upon heroic stories about children in the South during the 1950s and the early 1960s who had the courage to walk into previously all-white schools, guarded at times by federal marshals or police, and who defied the jeers and catcalls of white students and adults, overcame their own anxieties, and at length achieved what are presented to our students as enduring victories. These may be uplifting

JONATHAN KOZOL

stories but they also fail to give our kids the slightest
indication that most of the victories they celebrate
have, since that time, been cancelled out by more polite but no less implacable arrangements for the isolation of black children like themselves.

I think you were being very honest when you
said you feel as if you're lying to your children if you
leave these false impressions uncorrected and allow
the class, essentially, to swallow the idea that segregation is a shameful piece of distant history for which
our nation has absolved itself, rather than an ever-
present aspect of the lives they lead and education
they receive today.

"Here we are in a public school with not a single
white child in our class and only three white children
in the school's entire population. Hooray for Ruby
Bridges and for Linda Brown and all the other brave
black children of the South for having left us with a
legacy of social justice in our public schools, even if
this legacy has been completely, and intentionally,
ripped apart and shredded and abandoned in the
years since all the kids we teach today were born!"

I thought you were brave to say that to an audience of influential educators who have built their own
careers around "diversity instruction." I hope you
made them thoroughly uncomfortable.

I also think that you were right on target when
you said the way to honor heroes of the past isn't to
embalm their courage in a lesson plan of arm's-length
admiration but to *emulate* that courage by empowering

our students to see clearly and speak openly about the schools that they attend and neighborhoods in which they live right now. Otherwise, we place them in the strange position of believing that the unmistakable realities they see in school each day are somehow not to be believed and must be an incorrect perception or, if not a false perception, must be something that deserves a different name that carries no dishonor and bears no resemblance to the situation children of their race and age encountered 50 years ago.

The percentage of black children who now go to integrated public schools has fallen to its lowest level since the death of Dr. King in 1968. In New York and California, seven out of every eight black students presently attend a segregated school. In your school, as you have pointed out, as in almost every inner-city school I visit, white children make up only one or two percent of the enrollment.

Once, when I was in a class at P.S. 65, which was Pineapple's elementary school, I was surprised to see a white boy sitting in the second row, since I'd almost never seen another white child in the school. I asked the teacher how many white kids she had taught over the years. "I've been at this school for eighteen years," she said. "This is the first white student I have ever had!" It turned out he was an immigrant from Germany who had been assigned there by mistake. He had left the school before I visited again. The only other white child I had ever noticed in the school's enrollment of 800 students happened to be an immigrant as well. He was a kind and thoughtful Russian boy but he, too, departed rapidly.

In the elementary district that encompassed P.S. 65, there were only 26 white children in an overall enrollment of 11,000 students, which, according to my long division, comes out to a segregation rate of 99.8 percent—an improvement, if you want to call it that, of two tenths of one percentage point on the segregation rate in southern states a century ago.

The same scenario is seen in schools that serve black and Hispanic neighborhoods even in middle-sized and smaller cities. If I took a photo of the children that I meet in almost any of these schools, it would be indistinguishable from photos taken of the children in the all-black schools in Mississippi back in 1925 or 1930—precisely the same photos that are reproduced in textbooks now in order to convince our children of the moral progress that our nation has made since. Teachers "are participating in deception of their students," as you said up in Vermont, if these myths are not confronted and the truths that counter them are not presented to our children as a part of any course of study on "diversity."

Most of these inner-city schools, as you also pointed out, "don't simply make a mockery of *Brown v. Board of Education.*" They don't even live up to the promises of *Plessy v. Ferguson,* which stipulated back in 1896, as you said you felt you needed to remind your audience, that if our public schools were to be separate, "they must at very least be equal." It's a tribute to the awkward game that must be played in many school departments now that it takes a first grade teacher to spell out, and hammer out, the obvious to people who design curricula in history.

Admittedly, there are limits as to how far teachers ought to delve into these matters with a class of children who are only six years old. But even while employing wise discretion and while making full allowance for the fragile sensibilities of children who are still in the first grade, I think you're correct in saying that our teachers need to introduce a good big helping of political and intellectual irreverence into any lesson that might otherwise suggest to children in a classroom of contemporary racial isolation that they must discredit what they see before their eyes, with the result of teaching them to live with a peculiarly destructive lie.

At a New York City high school named for Dr. Martin Luther King, a classic segregated institution (96 percent black and Hispanic) in the middle of an affluent white section of Manhattan, students who apparently had thoroughly imbibed the lessons of their elementary grades went into the most remarkable contortions when I asked them if they thought it accurate to say that they were pupils in a "segregated" school. Indeed, the very introduction of that word seemed to surprise a number of the students in the ninth grade class that I was visiting. It was as if they'd never been invited by a teacher to consider this idea before.

"I don't think this is a segregated school," one student said, "because white students are allowed to come here. At least, if they want. . . ."

"Why don't they come here then?" I asked, noting that the neighborhood immediately around the school was home to thousands of white children.

"This school is *named* for Dr. Martin Luther King," another student said, wrestling oddly with the paradox this might present. But she seemed to work around that paradox in a surprising way. "I don't see how you could say this is a segregated school. Dr. King believed that every race is equal."

A few of the students launched into a heated disagreement with the students who had spoken first. "Hey!" said a tall black boy whose head was shaven and who told me that he once had been a student briefly at an integrated elementary school. "This right here"—he gestured to the students sitting all around him—"*this is it!* This is what it's all about." He wore an Army jacket and he had a look of shrewd impatience in his eyes. "This school is a segregated school. I don't think we need to dance around something so obvious."

A boy sitting next to him slapped his hand. "Thank you!" said a tall Hispanic girl who turned around to nod at him from the front row.

But some of the other students seemed affronted by his words and, oddly enough, appeared to be concerned that I might be offended somehow, even though I'd asked the question, by the slightly cutting way that he'd replied. I also had the clear impression that a number of the students felt it would be disrespectful of their school if they were to let themselves concede that what he said was true.

At that point, one of the older teachers in the room jumped into the argument and asked the students what exactly they believed Dr. King had been "about." All but a few of the answers she received were very vague—"we need to learn to get along with one another" and "respect our differences," "he was a man of peace," and other accurate but imprecise assertions that suggested they had never read a book on Dr. King, or one that presented an unsanitized account of his beliefs.

Later, in the hallway after class, the teacher vented her frustration that so many of these students had arrived in the ninth grade with virtually no knowledge of our nation's recent history. "If I'm teaching in a school named Martin Luther King," she told me, "I'm not going to come in and sugarcoat the things that he believed in. This is exactly the kind of institution he regarded as a moral wrong. Students who come here have a right to know this."

Some of my white friends in New York City take it as an act of incivility when I confront them with an angry statement like the one this teacher made or with the flat-out accusation that the student in the Army jacket voiced. Several of these friends of mine are liberals or, more accurately, former liberals who participated in some of the protests and the marches in the South during the 1960s but who now reject the practicality or, it seems, even the moral value of pursuing integration in the schools their own children attend.

Instead of conceding—even wistfully, regretfully—that racial segregation or, if they can't bear to bring themselves to speak those words, at very least near-total racial isolation is an accurate description of the status of most children in the education system in the city where they live, they bristle at this implication and appear to grant themselves some sort of ethical exemption by reminding me of all the decent things they did to help the cause of civil rights when they were young.

"I was at the March on Washington with Dr. King" is a familiar answer that I hear. Protest marches deeper in the South are also commonly recalled. Some recollect with pride that they were in the march across the fabled bridge in Selma, Alabama, which took place in 1965. I'm often struck by the nostalgia and authentic pride they seem to feel about those idealistic years in their own lives, which coincided with an idealistic era in our history. What is disturbing, nonetheless, is the apparent ease with which they use these memories to blind them to the more sophisticated system of apartheid in which they are, willingly or not, participating now.

Many black educators have expressed the same frustration you did when you spoke about the uses of the past as something like a piece of "meaningful but old and tattered cloth" that we have placed upon a shelf within a cupboard that we briefly open and then

carefully lock up again. I'd like to introduce you someday to an African-American teacher in New York who
told me once, during the time when I was working on
my book Amazing Grace, that he'd gotten to the point
where he confessed he couldn't "stand to hear about
the bridge at Selma, Alabama anymore" and refused
to give his kids a set of lesson plans he'd been assigned
for what he called "The Famous March Curriculum."
Instead, he said he'd posted on his classroom walls all
the stuff that he could find about the racist education
system in which he was working now.

"You see," he said, "to the very poor black children that I teach . . . , it doesn't matter much what
bridge you might have stood on thirty years ago.
They want to know what bridge you stand on now."

He was teaching older kids than you do. I'm not
sure what grade they were, but I thought of what he
said when you let me read the notes you typed up for
your presentation in Vermont. It seemed that all the
irritation you had felt exploded suddenly. In that moment, you weren't speaking merely as a teacher who's
been working her heart out every day to do the best
job that she can to serve the children in her class. You
were also speaking as a witness. I don't know if I would
say this to you if I didn't recognize how strongly you
believe it, but I think *all* teachers ought to feel the
right and have the courage to speak out as witnesses
to the injustices they see their children undergo. If we
won't speak out on these seemingly forbidden matters,
then who will?

But I also liked the fact that, even in the midst of all the indignation that you voiced, you did not leave out the sweetness and the many, many hours of sheer happiness you've known this year, as well as certain of the funny details you tucked in about the real life of a teacher in the elementary grades. I tried to imagine the reaction of the audience when you said that six-year-olds are "leaky little people" because of the many "accidents" they have. I wonder how many presentations made at education conferences ever mention matters quite so interesting as the great importance of the distance of the nearest bathroom from the classroom door. ("First graders leak!" as you explained this to me later, "either from their eyes" when they have painful quarrels with each other "or from their dribbly noses" when they're coming down with colds—or, as you put it, "from the other end more frequently.")

One of the reasons why I've found our conversations and our correspondence so refreshing is that you enjoy so much the small realities and daily misadventures, even the wet and messy ones, that take place in the classroom with your children. Even when you're speaking of school system policies that might leave another person sounding wilted by frustration, I notice that your voice still has that energetic sound of somebody who never lets herself be beaten down but keeps on coming back with a nice sense of lively combat, usually intermixed with pleasant bits of irony about the contradictions that you have to deal with.

I hope you won't mind this, but I told some

teachers in New York the anecdote you shared with me when you were working on the first report cards for your students. You said there was a box you had to check off that was labeled, "STUDENT IS RESPECT-FUL OF DIVERSITY." The teachers very much enjoyed your speculations about how to answer this.

First, you said, you toyed with the idea of filling in "Not Applicable." You said there was no way that you could honestly report that they had proven they might be respectful to another race of children whom they'd never had a chance to know. Then you said you thought of writing you were sure, because they're sensitive children, that they would respect the children of another race if Boston's schools "should someday figure out that it would be a good idea to let them meet such children" by allowing them to go to school together. I knew that in the end you wouldn't yield to the temptation to write either of these things, because you knew they might cause problems for your principal and certainly would make a few waves higher up in the administration if somebody in the school department happened to be told that you had done this. Teachers learn to choose which battles are worth fighting. This one obviously wasn't worth it.

Besides, I think that your impatience with the mis-use of that word, "diversity," and the whole surround-ing repertoire of watered-down discussion about civil rights, comes across to children in a number of more subtle ways. The intonations of your voice, a passing glance within your eyes in reaction to a passage in a story that you may be reading to the class, have their effect as well. The secret curriculum in almost any class, in my belief, is not the message that is written in a lesson plan or a specific book but the message of implicit skepticism or, conversely, of passivity or acquiescence that is written in the teacher's eyes and in the multitude of other ways in which her critical intelligence, her reservations about given truths, or else the absence of these inclinations and these capabilities, are quietly revealed.

Education, no matter what the rulebooks say, is never absolutely neutral. We either teach our children it's okay to write and talk about the things they think to be the truth or else we teach them that it's more acceptable to silence their beliefs, or even not to *have* beliefs but to settle for official truths that someone else has carefully prepared for them. A lot of those kids with whom I spoke at Martin Luther King School in New York had learned the second of these lessons far too well and long before they ever got to the ninth grade. The results were manifested in that muzzled consciousness in which they seemed to be entombed, that inability to scrutinize or speak about their own reality in thoughts or words that were their own.

I think we need to find the will to shatter this rock of silence starting at the earliest age possible. I wanted to cheer for you for having had the nerve to stand before an audience and say so!

CHAPTER EIGHT

Beware the Jargon Factory

Dear Francesca,

I liked your story about the woman whom you called "The Meta-Lady" who arrived to do a workshop with the teachers at your school last month. I gather she's been hired by the city to do workshops like this in a number of the elementary schools.

When the time reserved for "teacher input" came, you said you started telling her about a story that Shaniqua wrote about her grandma and the way the other children at her table had connected this to funny things that happened to their own grandmothers. You said the woman interrupted you at this point to inform you that you'd struck upon "a shrewd perception" that was more important than you seemed to understand. She said you had unwittingly arrived at what she called a "meta-concept." What the children at that

87

table had been doing, as she put it, was to make "a text-to-self connection."

I think you were justified in saying later that you thought that this was "gibberish." She had taken an ordinary reflex of the children—someone writes a story and the other children liken it to stories of their own—and had given it a big-time label which enabled her to slot it in a package of cognition theory that she seemed to think was more sophisticated than the way you had described it.

You said, "This woman really pissed me off," which isn't quite the elegant vocabulary Captain Black would probably expect from somebody named Lady Marmalade. But if this woman had talked to me the way she did to you, it would have pissed me off as well. It was her insistence that you did not realize what you had perceived that seems so grandiose and ignorant.

You said she then went on for well over an hour tacking on this prefix ("meta") to a bunch of other words, like "cognitive" and "strategy," explaining to you and the other teachers that this was a part of what she called "the newest research" about literacy education. You said the teachers were exchanging looks with one another and that one of them, your friend who teaches fifth grade, slipped out of the room at one point when she wasn't looking and did not come back.

These suddenly fashionable phrases seem to travel the rounds of education workshops with unusual rapidity. (It's also possible, I guess, that once we hear a term like this, we simply start to notice its recurrent use in other situations.) Only two weeks after you told me this, I was in Sacramento and the same term popped up once again during a luncheon I attended with a group of people who were working as curriculum advisers for the state. In answer to a question I had asked concerning classroom dialogue, a woman with a commanding presence who was sitting across the table from me gave me this reply: "We're speaking of a meta-moment taking place in interactional time."

The other people at the table seemed to be as baffled by these words as I was. They tried to change the subject to some other issue of importance they were dealing with. But she was insistent in her wish to keep on telling me about the value of these "meta-moments" and, try as they did, they could not shut her down.

This kind of jargon, which relies upon the pumping up of any simple notion by tacking on a fancy-sounding prefix or a needless extra syllable, infests the dialogue of public education nowadays like a strange syntactic illness that induces many educators to believe they have to imitate this language if they want to have a place in the discussion.

One of the most annoying consequences of this trend, as you've observed, is a peculiar tendency to use a polysyllabic synonym for almost any plain and ordinary word: "implement" for do, "initiate" for start, "utilize" for use, "identify" for name, "articulate" for

state, "replicate" for copy, "evaluate" for judge, "quan-
tify" for count, "strategize" for plan, "facilitate" for help,
"restructure" or "reconstitute" for change. The toss-in
use of adjectives like "positive" and "meaningful" (instead of, simply, "good" or "real") in front of nouns like
"outcome" or "collaboration" is another common way
of trying to pump extra air into a wilted and deflated
intellectual balloon.

Even a very good, time-honored word like "competence" is routinely decorated with a totally unneces-
sary extra syllable. "Competency" is the term one
hears ("competency-based instructional techniques"
has come to be a term of art) and frequently gets plu-
ralized to "competencies," yet another of those words
I know that you dislike because it sets our teachers up
for all those lists of mini-skills that boards of education
now churn out with regularity. Still, education writers
seem to find these phrasings irresistible. So there is a
bandwagon phenomenon. "Successful principals," we
are advised, "replicate best practices," "identify objectives," "initiate collaborative processes," "articulate
clear goals," and "evaluate results" that "impact student competencies and performance. . . ."

Once these words and phrases are disseminated
widely, they begin to be employed without much
thought by school officials and political appointees
who apparently believe the word or phrase itself will
lend significance to unexamined utterance. Not "big
words" in themselves, but big words that say nothing
more than little words could say, sometimes have the

added benefit of making a circular statement sound like a real idea.

In the presidency of George H. Bush, for instance, Education Secretary Lauro Cavazos, who had many difficulties in conveying an idea in simple words, told an audience that he could "quantitate the educational deficit" among the students in our schools and that this was why we needed to "restructure elementary and secondary education in this nation." What did the education secretary mean, exactly, by the word "restructure"? "By restructuring," he explained, "I mean developing and implementing strategies that will improve the educational process. . . ." At last, perhaps embarrassed to be using all these overloaded polysyllables in order to express a very small and commonplace idea, he said he was in favor of "curriculum reform that results in better education."

"What is school restructuring?" Kentucky's Board of Education asked in 1993.

"School restructuring," it offered in reply, "proceeds from a vision, goals, and a plan," is "systemic" but "at the same time a collaborative" and "intensely personal challenging process" and "creates new questions as a result of the process . . . ," is "always in an evolving state," and "is non-linear." I remember wondering why educated people could not set down their ideas about "restructuring" in language that displayed transparency of meaning and lucidity of thinking—qualities, I should think, good educators hope to inculcate in children.

One of the most prestigious national commissions, which it isn't in my interest to identify by name because I have friends who work there, tried its best to give a definition too. "School restructuring," said the commission, means "new ways to group students and to assess their progress through school-based management . . . , accountability, and a variety of strategies. . . ." Three specific stages of "restructuring" were then proposed. The first was "to reforge the sense of trust. . . ." The second: "To ensure that all students experience success . . . ," which requires that schools "need to be tracking the progress of each student." The third was to be sure that children see that "working hard in school" may be connected with "some future goal." Successfully restructured schools, the commission also noted, "identify strategies that lead to positive outcomes" and, at the secondary level, "focus on helping adolescents to use their minds. . . ."

These kinds of documents, devoid of grace or clarity or cleverness or beauty, are like wastelands of authoritative-sounding imprecision. The mechanistic clanking of those misappropriated verbs, the desperate reliance upon hyphenated phrases as the surrogates for actual connections between disparate ideas ("implementing outcome-based instruction in alignment with performance-based curricula"), the circularity of reasoning, the whole debilitating journey through an underbrush of tired words that have been used in documents like these a thousand times before, feels like the monologue of someone who has been depressed for decades.

You told me once how much you were affected by Paul Goodman's books when you were first exposed to them as a teenager. In speaking of the vague, unhappy somnolence of disaffected adolescents in one of his works—of "lively children brought to a pause," in his nicely chosen words—Goodman termed this dull sensation "Sunday-afternoon neurosis." And he said of those who suffer this experience, "Their hearts are elsewhere," but "they don't remember where." I think those words apply with equal force to many teachers who are asked to sit through workshops like the one that you reported with the "meta-lady" at your school.

Similar sessions take place at most regional and national conventions at which teachers, to be given credit for "professional development," are encouraged or required to sit in on workshops that are seldom taught by teachers who have first-hand understanding of the challenges they face but are often led by one of those ubiquitous consultants who appear predictably at these events and later make the rounds of local schools and districts.

I'm thinking, for example, of the "Efficacy Man" you spoke about with irritation after he had made a visit to your school and lectured you and all the other teachers in your building on the need for you to be "more efficacious" in "the strategies" you use. You said that when you asked him to explain these words in terms you could apply with your first graders, he shot you down by telling you that, if you even had to ask this question, you should not be teaching in a school for African-Americans! You said you were astounded at his rudeness but that this appeared to be part of "his shtick," his way of compensating for his inability to offer anything concrete or useful.

Teachers tell me that the same man, or another member of the "efficacy team" or of another "efficacy team"—I'm not sure how many groups like this there are—presents the same bombastic recipes at many regional conventions, where he tells them they must hold "high expectations" for their pupils, and "insist on competency-based instructional techniques" and, as a Chicago teacher added, "also strive for excellence." The teacher said she was embarrassed for his sake but could not suppress her anger at his condescending statements.

"The man is obviously brilliant!" said the teacher. "Until I heard him speak, these things would never have occurred to me. 'Excellence'—what a truly radical and mind-blowing idea! Here I am, a simple soul who had thought my purpose all these years had been to strive for mediocrity. . . ."

I have never heard this man, or anybody from "the efficacy team," so I can't vouch for what the teacher said. If you thought that there was any substance in the least in what you heard, I'd like to know. But I've sat through dozens of exhausting presentations made by similarly voluble performers in a period that stretches back some ten or fifteen years.

Sitting through some of those sessions in which overly assertive people were dispensing their prescriptive wisdom about "student-centered, multifaceted approaches" to "facilitate delivery" of this or to "restructure" that or to "impact" or "utilize" or "implement" whatever else, I used to feel a growing sense of desperation, like a thirsty person who is longing for a cool drink but is being handed glasses of dry sand. Since the jargon has an interlocking quality, however, those who use it seem to find it utterly coherent and convincing. To say that "school restructuring" means "implementing changes" for low-income children "in relation to their cohorts" by "insistence upon higher standards" comes to sound as if it tells us something we have never thought about before.

Many of the experts, corporate executives, and state or local school officials who participate in panels during these conventions know each other well by now and tend to throw these phrases back and forth to one another. An incestuous conviviality evolves between them—sorry, Francesca! I can see you smiling, but I don't know any other way to say this—based upon a common use of unassailable banalities. If one of them were suddenly impelled to stand up in impatience and say, "This is a whole lot of hogwash. None of us is saying anything that's new," it would have a ruinous effect by shattering the universe of language with more syllables than meaning.

You once jokingly suggested that we try to write a poem together using only words and phrases that are heard at education conferences or found in those official documents in which state standards are compiled. (I don't think it would be possible.) Perhaps another exercise that we might try would be to guess the probable reaction of a good clear-sighted poet such as William Carlos Williams or a plainspoken poet such as Robert Frost or, for that matter, W. H. Auden, who was so insightful when it came to matters of banality established as official language of the state, if they were alive today and could reflect upon the language being used, and propagated to our teachers, by so many of the experts who are being paid to raise the literacy levels of the nation.

All the "aints" and "don't nobody tell mes" and the pile-ups of "ands" and "buts" that Dobie used to use when he first came to you, and still uses when he's so inclined, do less damage to the English language than the kind of high-flown terminology your "meta-lady" tried to throw at you and which you had the good sense to reject.

Most teachers never talk to me this way once they escape these workshops and convention sessions and get back into their classrooms. If I'm visiting a school and ask a question to the teachers, for example, about textbooks or a reading method, most would feel embarrassed to reply, "I'm utilizing this . . ." or "implementing that. . . ." They use a normal word like "use" or "do" or "try." There are, it seems, two languages of public education. One of them is what I would call "expert talk" or "conference talk," and one is normal English. Some teachers learn to be adept at "conference talk" in order to protect themselves in public situations where they do not seem to think that their real voices will be heard and treated with respect. It always seems a diminution of themselves.

I'm not surprised that you have never let yourself be caught up in these ways of talking about education. You're fortunate, in more than one sense, that you came to public education from a literary background and had been immersed in the humanities and in a love of language in your high school years and, after that, in college. Not many teachers have been reading authors like Paul Goodman or the poetry of Yeats and Rilke since they were teenagers. I think this may have helped to immunize you against putting up with inauthentic words.

But even teachers who do not have literary backgrounds like your own, but who are thoughtful and well-educated people, with a normal sense of critical intelligence, instinctively reject these hyper-terminologies even if they use them when they must in order to defend their status as "professionals." And, of course, the seasoned veterans like Mr. Bedrock and Ms. Dukes have been teaching long enough to know how frequently the jargon and the "meta-phrases" of one decade disappear before the next round of official verbiage appears.

If we want to teach our children to take pride in

their own voices, I think that teachers need to fight hard to take pride in their own voices too. The jargon factory in education is a very busy place and it will doubtless keep on churning out new words and phrases that are no less cumbersome, or lacking in substantial meaning, than the ones in use today. To use one of those lovely words your former student liked, we need to encourage future teachers not to be bamboozled. Reject the clankety vocabularies. Defend the freshness of your voice. Defend its authenticity.

CHAPTER NINE

Aesthetic Merriment

"Wiggly" and "Wobbly" and "Out!"

Dear Francesca,

I promised I would think about the question that you asked me in the playground of your school the other day after the children were dismissed and most of them had already gone home. Shaniqua and another child were still waiting for their mothers and were studying some kind of very big and ugly-looking bug they had discovered crawling on a spot of grass that had appeared as the snow was melting.

While you were watching them you asked me whether anyone I know who's setting education policy these days ever speaks about the sense of fun that children have, or ought to have, in public school or the excitement that they take when they examine interesting creatures such as beetle-bugs and ladybugs and other oddities of nature that they come upon—

or even merely whether they are happy children and enjoy the hours that they spend with us in school.

The truth is that in all the documents I read that come from Washington or from the various state capitals, or from the multitude of government-supported institutes where goals are set and benchmarks for performance of our students are spelled out in what is usually painstaking detail, I never come on words such as "delight" or "joy" or "curiosity" or, for that matter, "kindness," "empathy," "compassion for another child." Nothing, in short, that would probably come first for almost any teacher working with young children.

There is no "happiness index" for the children in our public schools, and certainly not for children in the inner-city schools where happiness is probably the last thing on the minds of overburdened state officials. Perhaps there ought to be. The school boards measure almost every other aspect of the lives our children lead in school but never ask if they look forward to the days they spend with us.

Fortunately, there are many teachers who, no matter what the pressures that the states and federal government impose, refuse to banish these considerations and, by their nature, could not do so even if they tried. I told you once of a young teacher whom I met some years ago in the South Bronx whose name was April Gamble, a perfect name, I thought, for someone in the springtime of her life who was starting out on her career in the third grade. Her students had sent me one of those fat envelopes of friendly letters children sometimes send to writers, asking if I'd visit them someday when I was in their neighborhood. One of the children wrote, "My name is Pedro. I am 7 years old. Would you come and visit us for 6 hours so we could tell you everything about our life?" He signed his letter, "From my heart to my eyes, Pedro."

I couldn't resist those invitations, so one day I called the principal and went to meet the class. Pedro happened to be sick that day, so I didn't get to meet him. But I got to know some of the other children in the classroom pretty well and later kept in touch with them.

At one point in the morning, the discussion I was having with the children got a little out of hand—you've noted that this happens to me now and then—and the teacher realized that I wasn't sure how I should handle things. She seemed to know exactly what to do.

She rose to her feet and put one hand, with fingers curled up slightly, just beneath her mouth, and curled her other hand in the same way but held it out about twelve inches to the right. I watched with fascination as the class subsided from the chaos I'd created and the children stood and did the same thing Mrs. Gamble did. All these children with one hand before their mouth, one to the side, and with their eyes directed to the teacher. What was this about?

Then the teacher started humming softly. Then she briefly trilled a melody in her soprano voice, and some of the children started trilling their own voices too. And suddenly I understood: It was an orchestra, and they were the flute section! In their hands were the imaginary flutes. Their little fingers played the notes and when the teacher bent her head as if she were so deeply stirred by the enchanted music she was hearing that she had to tilt her body in response, the children bent their bodies too.

The principal, who was standing in the doorway, seemed to be as fascinated by the sight of this as I was. I could see that she admired Mrs. Gamble as a teacher but was obviously taken also by the sweetness of her manner—the precision of her fingers on the keys! And then the teacher danced a bit from foot to foot before the children and I thought of Papageno and Tamino and the lovely tune Tamino plays in Mozart's Magic Flute; and the children danced from foot to foot as well. And then the music ended and the teacher put away her flute with an efficient and conclusive motion of her hands and all the children did the same and we began our class discussion once again.

What I remembered later wasn't only an effective trick for bringing third grade children who had grown a trifle wild back into a calm and quiet state of mind. It was also the impromptu dance the teacher did, only a step or two, but just enough to fill the moment with gratuitous amusement so that, even in regaining grown-up governance over those joyful little protons and electrons that I'd inadvertently set into motion, she also showed herself to be a woman who was not too overly "mature," or too "professional," to show the happiness she felt at making magic music for the children with a magic, and imaginary, flute.

When Mrs. Gamble trilled her voice and ran her fingers through the air, she didn't simply play the flute. She also played the playfulness within herself and seemed to play the spirits of the children too. She later told me that one third of all the children in her class, and in the school, suffered from asthma, which was common in the South Bronx as a consequence of New York City's policy of placing toxic installations like waste burners in the neighborhood. You wouldn't have guessed it on that morning. For a minute there, we might have been a thousand miles from the city in a magic forest where the evening air smells fresh and green and not one of the spirits of the woods has any trouble breathing.

I've watched other teachers use their own inventive ways to spice the schoolday for their children with brief words and moments that are like their evanescent tributes to the need for impulse and for beauty in the classroom. This doesn't mean that they ignore the necessary skills they need to teach but that they feel the confidence to interweave the teaching of those skills into a context of aesthetic merriment that satisfies and does not enervate the children's sense of curiosity and joy.

I remember a first grade class in Minnesota where the bookshelves and the color-coded reading bins were filled with hundreds of children's books and stories, organized according to the levels of ability they would require for a child to understand them. Books on bears and worms and caterpillars had positions of particular distinction in the sun-filled corner room in which the class took place. The Very Hungry Caterpillar and some of the other works of Eric Carle were favorites of the children; and for a memorable period of time they had their own real caterpillar in the room, a "woolly bear caterpillar," as these six-year-old researchers ascertained with some assistance from their teacher.

On the day the teacher brought him into school, all other class activities came to a halt for a good period of time. He was a beautiful creature, with rich brown and orange hair that looked like fur, and in the weeks that followed, children often slipped out of their chairs to pet him softly with their fingers or simply to study him with wonderment.

The day he disappeared into the gray cocoon that he was spinning was, of course, momentous for the children too. And when he at length emerged as a very splendid tiger moth and the teacher opened the window and he flew away one April afternoon, celebratory rites were held for him but were followed by a study of life cycles among caterpillars and additional small members of his species.

I used the word "wonderment" in speaking of the feelings that the presence of this caterpillar had awakened in the children. That's another word you seldom find in any of those documents that tabulate the items of essential knowledge children are supposed to learn

LETTERS TO A YOUNG TEACHER

in order to assume their place someday, as we are told, in the national economy and help to "sharpen our competitive edge" in "the global marketplace." (I actually saw a "mission statement" with those words posted in an inner-city elementary school not long ago. Why on earth should kids in elementary school be asked to care about their future role within the global marketplace? Why should teachers foist this mercenary nonsense on them in the first place?)

I loved the reflections that you sent me on the role of whim and wonderment within the classroom. "If at the end of the day," you said, "I find Arturo standing at the window instead of reading at his seat," and if you notice that he's "wide-eyed" and "entranced" by looking at a squirrel in a tree, you said you would not call to him "to sit down and pick up his book." In fact, you said, "I might even join him there" in order to remember what it feels like to be young enough to take so much amazement in a squirrel. "I won't be responsible," you wrote, "for hurrying my children out of that age when many things are interesting and so much is new."

Even in the presentation of mandated lessons, I've noticed that you try hard to adapt them with a sense of playfulness to the concerns that have immediate connections with your children's lives. The last time I visited your class, I saw a timeline posted on the wall above the reading rug. I know that timelines are a commonplace device that first grade teachers use to introduce their students to a recognition of progressions

105

from one day or month or season to the next. But this was no commonplace variety of timeline. I would call it "a timeline with a sense of humor."

In fact, as I remember this, it wasn't even called a timeline. It was called a "Tooth Line," as the sign you'd written just above it read. Very convincing-looking teeth, which I think you said that you had cut out of a piece of cardboard, had been placed in little slots along the left side of a sheet of something that resembled fiber-board. All the children in the class could find their own teeth somewhere in one of those slots. I saw "Shaniqua's Tooth," "Arturo's Tooth," "Dobie's Tooth," et cetera.

At the top of the chart you had created four "tooth-status" columns. The first column was for teeth that hadn't yet come loose. The second column was for "Wiggly Teeth," the third for "Wobbly Teeth." The fourth column was for teeth that had come "Out!" (I liked the exclamation point you put there because it's a big event for children when they finally lose a tooth, whether or not they get rewarded every time with a quarter or a dollar underneath their pillow.)

As children reported on the status of a tooth, their cardboard tooth would be advanced across the chart to "Wiggly Teeth," then "Wobbly Teeth," then "Out!" The thing about this timeline that I think had caught the fancy of the children was not only that it had been built upon a series of events that obviously matter very much to six-year-olds but also that it clearly had been done with a degree of frolicsome intent. "Wiggly" and "wobbly" are fun to say. They're slightly silly-sounding words. I wouldn't be surprised if that's one reason why you picked them.

The teaching of sequences, progressions, categories is, I know, a very important part of early education. But, as you demonstrated in this instance, there's no reason why these concepts must be taught in shopworn terms that are external to the students' lives. Immediacy, and a sense of fun in the immediate, can infiltrate the teaching of these concepts too.

The march of little teeth across that chart was, in itself, inherently amusing. When I asked one of the children which one was her tooth, she went right up and pointed to it. "This one is *my* tooth," she said, then stuck her fingers in her mouth to show me which one of her teeth it was. On the chart it said that it was "wiggly," but after she had moved it around awhile with her forefinger and thumb, she took the cardboard tooth out of its slot and slipped it into "wobbly." I know that you like to have the children do these things collectively when everyone is seated on the rug. I guess I should have told her to hold off and do it the next morning, but she did it out of impulse.

Francesca, I know this letter, like some others I've been writing to you recently, is proving to be more rambling than I intended it to be. But if there's a common theme in all of this, it has to do with the upholding of a sense of artistry and imaginative creativity on the part of teachers at a time when both are under serious assault. A couple of years ago, a high official in the U.S. Department of Education said that the objective of the White House was "to change the face of reading instruction across the United States from an art to a science," a statement that could not have brought much comfort to those teachers who believe that books have more to do with artistry than metrics and that teaching children how to read them calls for somewhat different skills than teaching physics or geometry.

But this longing to turn art to science, as it turned out, didn't stop with reading methodologies. In many schools, it now extends to almost every aspect of the schoolday and the lives that children lead within it. Artistry and furry caterpillars do not stand much of a chance against these cold winds blowing down from Washington. All the more reason, then, for teachers to resist these policies and to use their ingenuity in every way they can to undermine the consequences of this pseudoscientific push for uniformity.

In a class in North Carolina that I visited last year, the teacher had tacked up a pleasantly defiant poster on one of the classroom walls. "How to Be an Artist" was the heading. "Stay loose, learn to watch snails, plant impossible gardens . . . , make friends with freedom and uncertainty, look forward to dreams. . . ."

The teacher didn't slight the basic skills. Her low-income students did okay on their exams. But when I asked about the reading method she was using, whether every aspect of her reading lessons was prescribed for her or whether she was free to innovate in any ways at all, she shook her head like someone who was shaking off an irritant—a flea or a mosquito.

"I like to mix it up!" she said and tossed her long hair gleefully, then pivoted around to keep an eye on one of the rambunctious boys sitting in the back part of the room.

I like the way you "mix it up" as well. I hope that many other teachers coming into urban schools will feel the wish to do the same. Down with concerns about "the global marketplace!" Up with "Wiggly" and "Wobbly" and "Out!" Childhood does not exist to serve the national economy. In a healthy nation, it should be the other way around. We have a major battle now ahead of us, not just about the tone and style of a child's education but about the purposes it should espouse and whether we, as teachers, need to go down on our knees before a brittle business-driven ethos that is not our own. We need the teachers who are coming to our classrooms making up their minds, before they even get here, which side they are on.

CHAPTER TEN

High-Stakes Tests and Other Modern Miseries

Dear Francesca,

I hate to have to switch gears from the magic music played by children and their happy teacher on imaginary flutes to the miseries of high-stakes testing, which is growing more relentless and obsessive in the inner-city schools with every passing year. But you have told me several times how much this troubles teachers at your school, and other teachers in the larger districts that I visit speak of it repeatedly. They tell me that these tests, which, as you know, must now be given every year beginning in third grade at the insistence of the federal government, have started to create an atmosphere of high anxiety, almost a sense of siege mentality, within their schools.

The same tests, of course, are given in suburban schools as well, because the federal law applies to every public school in the United States. But in most suburban schools, where students tend to do well on these standardized exams, principals and teachers do not feel the pressure to distort curriculum and resort to other drastic measures to protect their schools from federal sanctions when the test scores of their students are released each year.

It's a different story in too many inner-city schools, especially the ones that have been labeled "low-performing" for historically high rates of failure. If these congenitally underfunded schools don't post the gains the government demands, they face a series of penalties, including loss of funds, so that the schools with fewest resources will end up with even less. And if their rate of progress isn't fast enough to satisfy the government, they also have to pay for private test-prep corporations to come into school and drill their students for the next set of exams—more money for testing, less money for instruction.

In order to avoid these penalties, principals have often been reduced to taking measures which they tell me privately that they abhor. Thousands of inner-city elementary schools, for instance, have dramatically cut back the time permitted for instruction in the content areas—science, social studies, literature, and the arts (the arts themselves have been abandoned almost totally in many of these schools)—in order to create long periods of time, typically at least a quarter of the year, in which the children can be drilled on strategies to try to boost their scores.

At P.S. 65, when Pineapple was there, fifth grade teachers had to set aside all other lessons for two hours every morning, and then again for the final hour of the day, to drill the children for their tests for three months prior to exams. On top of this, two afternoons a week, children had to stay from 3:00 p.m. to 5:00 p.m. for yet another session of test-drilling, and on Saturdays they had to come to school again for three additional hours of the same routine during the final four weeks just before exams.

There was no pretense that these drilling sessions held the slightest bit of educative value for the students. If this had been the principal's belief, she would not have limited these sessions only to the weeks and months just prior to exams. If test-drilling were regarded as a valuable portion of instruction, it would have been given to all children in the school throughout the course of the entire year. The reason this was not done was that nobody believed test-drilling was of educative worth. Its only function was to skew the scores, defend the school from state or federal punishments, and, as many of the teachers at the school believed, enhance the reputation of the principal.

In order to gain extra time to prep their students for exams, some urban districts have, in recent years, gone to the extreme of taking recess from their children. In Atlanta, schools have been intentionally constructed with no playgrounds, so that no time can be wasted on activities that will not raise the scores.

Chicago has largely abolished recess too; the only exceptions that I know are some high-scoring schools, mostly in affluent communities.

In other districts, standardized exams are now administered to children in their kindergarten year, sometimes beginning in the first weeks of the fall, in order, as the principals say, "to get them ready" for the tests that lie ahead. Children of that age, unless they've had the opportunity for preschool, usually do not yet know that pages run from left to right. (You've told me that Arturo, the child whom you called your "little bear," didn't know this basic information when he started first grade with you last September.) Many kindergarten children haven't yet learned how to hold a crayon or a pencil. They look at these tests in terror. They start to cry. They pee in their pants. The teacher's not allowed to help them other than by offering some faint encouragement: "Keep going. The whole page. All by yourself. . . ."

Some of these districts have gone to the additional extreme of refusing to let kindergarten children have their "nap time" any longer, so that teachers can carve out an extra 30 minutes or an hour every day to prepare them for their tests. "If the state is holding us accountable" for raising scores, an official in one of these districts said, "this is the way we have to do it. Kindergarten is not like it used to be."

If at least these kids had had some years of preschool education they might have a better chance of coping with these tests when they are five or six years old. But most of the low-income children in these schools have had no pre-K education, largely because of the underfunding of the federal Head Start program by the very government that now insists these children must be rigorously judged and tested. Nearly a million of our nation's poorest three-to-five-year-olds are denied even a single year of Head Start—a good many more than the number who receive it. And even though a number of states claim to offer universal preschool programs for their children, only in rare cases are these claims to be believed. In New York, for instance, an inaccurately titled program known as "Universal Pre-K" turns out, despite its name, to serve only a quarter of the four-year-olds within the state.

Meanwhile, at the opposite extreme, children of the upper-middle class are typically placed in rich developmental pre-K programs starting as early as the age of two and, depending on the month their birthday falls, may receive as many as three years of very solid and expensive preschool education. (In New York, the most prestigious preschools, which are called "the Baby Ivies," cost as much as $22,000 for a full-day program.)

A few years later, when they get to the third grade, all of these children, rich and poor, are forced to take the same high-stakes exams, which in many districts now determine whether they will be promoted or held back. I don't think it comes as much of a surprise to any teacher to discover which ones tend to score the highest and are slotted into programs for "the talented and gifted"—the initial stage in a long series of predictable advantages that will lead them in their secondary years to be assigned to Honors classes and A.P.—and which ones are most likely to score far below grade level and may therefore find themselves subjected to the penalty of nonpromotion. To me, Francesca, there's something deeply hypocritical in a society that holds a child only eight or nine years old accountable for her performance on a high-stakes standardized exam but does not hold the Congress and the president accountable for robbing her of what they gave their own kids six or seven years before.

In any event, the tests are there; and whether they're introduced in kindergarten or a few years later in third grade, the better teachers in these schools detest the rote-and-drill routines that have been put in place, "aligned," as it is said, with items to be measured by those tests. The less creative, more robotic teachers don't object so heatedly to this agenda, which leaves almost nothing to the teacher's competence or her imagination. The less of the life of the mind a teacher brings into the classroom, the less that teacher has to forfeit when she gives in to these anti-intellectual techniques.

As you know, Francesca, I recruit young teachers every time I have the chance when I speak at colleges and universities. I never recruit people who seem docile, flat-natured, and boring. If they're boring to a grown-up, it seems likely they'll be boring to a class

116

of children too. But if they're dynamic and engaging individuals, if they're in love with children and in love with language and like to read good books and poetry and talk about them with excitement, and if their heads seem thoroughly screwed on, so I feel assured about their personal stability—in other words, if they're the kind of person you'd be eager to have as an intern in your class—I always say, "Come on! Wrap up the courses that you need in order to be certified. Then bring your interesting personality, your energy, your love of beauty, and the academic benefits of your good education into the schools where people with your gifts are needed most."

What happens to these teachers when they come into one of these heavily test-driven schools?

One of the first things they discover is that they cannot just walk up to the chalkboard on a Monday morning and write out in big bold letters as the outcome of a lesson: "Today I read my favorite poem of William Butler Yeats, or Gwendolyn Brooks, or Langston Hughes, to my third graders and discovered that they loved it!" No, that kind of outcome will not be regarded as acceptable. What children love or do not love has no role at all within the world of tough and testable accountability. Instead, if the teacher wants to read a poem she loves, she has to manipulate it somehow to pretend that it belongs in one of those compartments of officially ordained proficiency that we have talked about before. "I used"—or, preferably, "utilized"—"a poem by William Butler Yeats to deliver the following three state proficiencies" that will be measured on exams. And she also has to put those state proficiencies right up there on the board, and put official numbers from the standards guidelines next to them, so that the skills that she "delivers" will be easily identified by any of those middle-level supervisors— "curriculum cops," as teachers call them—who stop by from time to time to check on her.

Even the stories and the dialogue found in those children's classics most of us grew up to love— the mystical adventures and the soft epiphanies of Pooh and Piglet, for example, or Eeyore's sorrowful pronouncements—cannot be presented simply as the literary treasures that they are but have to be treated as a kind of "quarry" from which numbered state proficiencies (or "competencies") can be hacked out and held up to the bright light of curricular illumination. The charm and innocence of the story can't be valued for themselves. Instead, they have to be exploited for an external purpose. So, apart from all the other thefts they undergo, children in these schools are robbed of any understanding that the reason, certainly the best of reasons, human beings read books is for the pleasure that they give us.

School officials pay lip-service now and then to the worth of learning "for its own sake." But these statements do not hold up very well in schools where kids are being told it's not just important that they pass their tests but, as a teacher at one New York City school observed to me, that "passing this—the test—is actually the only thing that *is* important." When teachers have to underline this point by sticking Pooh and Piglet with official numbers that connect them to the items on a state examination, the message becomes utterly indelible.

I've noticed you refuse to put the standards postings with their numbers on your walls. You said that you'd feel stupid "putting up a bunch of numbers" for no other reason than "to cover my rear end." More teachers than not who work in urban schools do not feel emboldened to dismiss these regulations quite so easily.

I was stopped cold one day in the South Bronx when I saw the following outcome written on the blackboard of a third grade class: "English Language Arts No. E-2, [subtopic] D . . . The student will produce a narrative procedure." When I later asked the teacher what it meant, he showed at least that he had a sense of humor and he laughed about the phrase. "It just means to write a story," he replied. I asked him what would happen to him if he used those words instead of the elaborate phrase he'd written on the board. He gave me a shrewd and knowing look. "You have to use the language of the standards."

I told him that "producing a procedure" sounded kind of strange to me. The two words didn't seem to go with one another. "It's horrible syntax. I agree," he answered without any hesitation. I didn't even ask about the posting of the number. I knew he considered it a waste of time but felt he had no choice but to comply.

The scripted lessons that he had to teach, like other scripted programs you and I have talked about, relied upon a rapid-fire series of short questions he was forced to ask and already-scripted answers that the children were expected to provide. In dozens of cities, similar methods are mandated now for black and Hispanic children who attend the lowest-scoring schools. They're used in major districts like Chicago and Los Angeles and in smaller districts such as Hartford, and right here in Lawrence, Massachusetts, which, I think you know, is overwhelmingly minority.

If these methods actually worked, much as I dislike them, I might put aside my reservations (I know you'd be very disappointed if I did this) and I might say, "Okay, do them if you have to." The trouble is, they do *not* work except for the lowest-scoring children in a class, and, even then, the gains that they achieve sustain themselves for only a brief period of time. These are testing gains, not learning gains. If they were learning gains, they would persist into the secondary grades; but I have followed many of these children into middle school, and then into their high school years, and seen how rapidly these artificial gains evaporate.

"Scores up for minority children in their fourth grade tests!" newspaper headlines periodically report when there's been a modest upward blip in test results in any given year. But I meet the same kids four years later in eighth grade and find that most of them can't write a cogent sentence and can't comprehend a simple text. Some of them are able to sound out the words phonetically, but when they read a text aloud they read in droning voices without affect or the slightest evidence of understanding. They sound like plastic people reading plastic words but not ideas.

As middle school teachers also note to their frustration, many of these kids cannot constructively participate in class discussions because they have never learned in elementary school to ask discerning questions or to analyze or criticize complex ideas. The children of the suburbs learn to think and to interrogate reality; the inner-city kids meanwhile are trained for nonreflective acquiescence. One race and social class is educated for the exploration of ideas and for political sagacity and future economic power; the other is prepared for intellectual subordination. The longer this goes on, Francesca, I'm afraid the vast divide that we already see within American society is going to grow wider.

The advocates for these approaches have now been in power and have had their way in shaping urban education for a lengthy period of years. Some of these practices, indeed, preceded the passage of the federal law No Child Left Behind and took effect in cities like New York as long ago as 1995. Yet, after all these years of hype and sloganeering and exhausting incantations—"All kids have potential!" "Every child can achieve!"—and all these years of verbal bloat and bombast on the part of those who market rote-and-drill instruction with the same exaggerated claims as those who market miracle weight-loss programs on late-night TV, the average black and Hispanic twelfth grade student reads at the level of the typical seventh grade white student.

Even this statistic, devastating as it is, probably understates the learning gap for students in the secondary years, because so many black and Hispanic students disappear from school before their senior year and therefore aren't included in these numbers. For black males in particular, noncompletion rates have not merely "not improved" but seem to have worsened somewhat in these years. In New York City and Chicago, which together enroll 10 percent of all the black male students in the nation, more than 70 percent of those who enter ninth grade fail to finish twelfth grade in four years, and most of the overage boys who do not make it in four years are likely never to graduate at all.

These are not just bad statistics; they are plague statistics. Those who believe that high-stakes testing and the methods of instruction, modeled upon B. F. Skinner's work in rat psychology, that it has forced on many inner-city schools are an effective substitute for equal opportunity have had their chance to prove that they know something that the rest of us do not know; but they have failed in this. They have been proven wrong.

The terrible losses children of color have incurred during these recent years are seen most vividly at the nation's most distinguished secondary schools such as the very famous and highly selective Stuyvesant High School in New York, where black enrollment constituted 13 percent of the student body at the beginning of the 1980s but today is a humiliating 2 percent. More to the point, since we're talking about testing, during the period since relentless test-drill regimens went into effect in the elementary schools that serve the city's poorest and most deeply segregated children, the number of black students getting into Stuyvesant has dropped by half. Do advocates for high-stakes testing ever sit down and thoughtfully reexamine their ideas? It seems that they do not.

President Bush and his advisers, during his first term in office, sometimes used to charge that teachers who oppose these testing policies do so out of fear of being judged on their success or failure and that this, rather than intelligent and ethical reflection, is the reason why they are "opposed to accurate assessment" of their pupils, as the White House frequently alleged. The recklessness of this accusation is a classic instance of the uninformed contempt with which the president appeared to view the teachers of our nation. The truth is that most teachers in our public schools are not "opposed to testing," just so long as the tests they give are genuinely diagnostic and enable them to pinpoint areas where children have the greatest needs. But this is not the case with high-stakes tests, which tell us almost nothing that's directly relevant and helpful to an individual child but are used instead to paste a retroactive label of "success" or "failure" on a child, class, or an entire school collectively.

Last month, I watched you give a diagnostic test in which you were sitting down beside one of the children and keeping a running record of her areas of weakness so, as you explained to me, you could come back and focus on those weaknesses in later periods of individual instruction. There was absolutely nothing in this process to intimidate the child. Instead, she seemed delighted to be able to have so much time alone with you. And, unlike the standardized exams mandated by the state, the test did not subtract time from instruction, because it was a portion of instruction. Both you and the child learned while you were doing this.

I've watched teachers in suburban schools giving exactly the same test to their first graders. Again, the process was inherently instructive and relaxed; there was no tension or anxiety attached to "the results." And those results, moreover, were immediately useful, which is not the case with standardized examinations, a point of which some of the die-hard advocates for these examinations seem to be strangely unaware.

"All we want to do," they say, "is to help the teacher recognize the problems that her students face so she can place a greater emphasis on areas where more attention is required." It's hard to figure out how isolated from the real world of the classroom high officials of the government must be when they make statements of this sort. In most districts, high-stakes tests are given in the end of winter, but the teachers never see the scores their kids receive in time to be of any use to them because the scores don't usually come back, at earliest, until the final weeks of June. (In New York, I've been with a principal in mid-July when she got her first look at the scores on tests that had been given five months earlier. In a number of urban districts, scores on an examination given in the winter have not been received until the end of August.) What is a teacher supposed to do at this point? Send her kids a bunch of postcards telling them that they weren't trying hard enough in the preceding winter?

The same sense of being out of touch, of having little first-hand knowledge of what takes place in the schools themselves, comes across in several of the other routine accusations we are hearing from conservatives. Many of those, for instance, who incorrectly charge that teachers for the most part are opposed to any form of testing in the public schools also make the incorrect assumption that most teachers are opposed to making use of phonics as one portion of instruction. This is, indeed, an accusation that has taken on almost liturgical importance among critics of our public schools.

"Phonics" is a magical word in the thinking of conservatives; but, as you know, Francesca, this is another reckless accusation, since the vast majority of teachers in our elementary schools consider a well-organized and consistent emphasis on phonics to be not merely useful but essential in those cases where a child truly needs it. The teachers who are willing to work hardest, and to put in the most time in preparation, learn how to extract their phonics lessons from the initial writings of their pupils or from the story-and-picture books their students are attracted to, rather than rely upon the pit-pat phonics scripts that isolate phonetic skills from any context that has meaning or holds interest for a child; but this does *not* mean they reject a systematic use of phonics where it is of value.

In most of the better elementary schools I visit, there is a delicate balance between teaching children to decode phonetically, developing their comprehension skills, exposing them to good, enticing literary works, and encouraging their early efforts to set down their own ideas in words. What young teachers will discover rapidly, however, is that there is a large and highly vocal group of advocates for phonics who have no interest in such balance but who are convinced that phonics in and of itself represents some kind of bitter medicine that every child must be forced to swallow, whether he or she already knows the basic consonant and vowel sounds or not.

I think I told you once about one of these people, whom I call "the evangelical believers," a woman well past middle age who claimed, quite inexplicably, that she was a fan of mine and managed to show up at almost any lecture that I gave in Phoenix or at the nearby university in Tempe. At the end of my talk, no matter what the subject might have been, she would approach me and chastise me for not having recognized that phonics was the only real solution to whatever problem I'd described. She did this once even at the end of a talk I gave on homelessness! My research assistant, to whom she wrote repeatedly after I became exhausted from replying to her long handwritten letters, called her "The Phonetic Fanatic from Phoenix." But, no matter how discouraging we tried to be, she kept on writing to us anyway.

Much of the contemporary pressure upon urban teachers to "do phonics" to the virtual exclusion of all other aspects of instruction in the language arts originates in a postmodern version of the same fanaticism. Balanced approaches like the one you use, and which is supported by your principal, are regarded by the strict phonetics advocates as "unscientific," "too informal," and "not research-based." (I also get the sad impression sometimes, when I hear the sternness in their words, that almost any method of instruction children actually enjoy is, for this reason, automatically distrusted; but that's a separate issue altogether.)

There's a final point you raised in your last letter, a blasphemous point given the views that are ascendant now in Washington and in most state capitals. This is the whole business of the intellectual authority that is attributed by many of the high officials in our urban schools to the entire body of materials that are being turned out by the standards-writers and technicians of accountability.

Most of these materials, as you slyly surmised, are written not by seriously respected scholars or by wise and venerated teachers but by fairly undistinguished semi-intellectuals who would seldom qualify for tenure at a first-rate university. The clunkety prose, the reliance upon arbitrary overstatement, and the seemingly obsessive need to fit all pieces of the learning process into namable compartments are not the characteristics of capacious intellectuals. Wise philosophers, good scientists or poets, gifted mathematicians, accomplished literary critics, or reputable specialists in children's psychological development would not likely be disposed to spend long hours of their time in numbering and naming isolated particles of balkanized cognition that usually have only forced connections with each other and, most often, no connection with the context of our children's lives. Standards compilations tend to be, exactly as you stated it, "the products of the dutiful but uninspired."

Teachers who are coming for the first time into inner-city schools need to be well armed with the same level of self-confidence that has enabled you to see these standards compilations, and the testing superstructure they support, with the healthy dose of skepticism they deserve. Ernest Hemingway's raw-edged, somewhat blustery remark that writers need good "shit detectors" when they look at their own work might usefully be paraphrased to say that teachers need the same tough critical capacity when reading through the mountains of state documents and test-related federal mandates that are handed out to them and often end up spilling off their kitchen tables late at night when all they really want to do is to prepare good lessons for their classes the next morning.

I do agree, Francesca, with the realistic point you made that teachers who oppose the high-stakes testing regimens, no matter how intense their feelings, do not have the right to simply "shut the whole thing from their minds," because their students, as you put it, "will be judged and sorted" by the scores that they receive. So here, as in so many other situations teachers face, they have to balance some of their most deeply held convictions against the practical necessity of defending students from the punishments and stigma that the educational establishment seems all too willing to dole out to them.

Still, tests, as every educator knows, do not teach reading, writing, or the other basic elements of subject matter; only good hard-working teachers do, and only if they work under conditions that respect their own intelligence and do not try to rob them of their own identities by forcing the junk-lexicon of "systems experts" down their throats. Teachers have to find the will to counteract this madness. At very least, they ought to make it clear to every child in their room that high-stakes testing is, at best, a miserable game we're forced to play but that our judgment of our students' intellect and character and ultimate potential will have no connection with the numbers tabulated by a person who is not an educator, and has never met them, working in a test-score factory 1,000 or 3,000 miles away.

I don't like to say something so harsh, but if teachers cannot figure out a way to do this, it is possible that they should not remain within the classroom. Abject capitulation to unconscionable dictates from incompetent or insecure superiors can be contagious. We should not permit this habit to be passed on to our children.

CHAPTER ELEVEN

The Single Worst, Most Dangerous Idea

Education Vouchers and the Privatization of Our Public Schools

Dear Francesca,

In one of your recent letters you referred to high-stakes testing as "a kind of shaming ritual" which you said you were convinced is not intended to improve the public schools but is being used, instead, as a dramatic way by which "to expose them to sustained humiliation" and to cast doubt, in this manner, on the whole idea of public education as a proper instrument by which to serve the public's need.

I agree with you on this. I don't think it's a coincidence that standardized examinations of a highly punitive and judgmental character have often been promoted most aggressively by those who also favor market competition in the educational arena, with the ultimate objective of establishing a universal voucher system in this nation.

Vouchers, in my own belief, represent the single worst, most dangerous idea to enter education discourse in my lifetime. The strongest advocates for this idea are very clear in stating their contempt for public education, which they term a "Soviet" or "socialistic" system and which they are eager to replace by a system in which public dollars would not go to schools themselves but would be assigned instead to individuals who would then be free to spend them either at a public school or at a private institution.

Voucher advocates, for now, place most of their emphasis on children living in the neighborhoods of greatest poverty where the failure levels in the public schools are very high, since they know that their appeal would be rejected by most parents in suburban areas where schools are adequately funded and where kids, in general, do reasonably well. Having narrowed their appeal to those whose children undergo the classic consequences of unequal segregated education—an injustice that proponents of a voucher system have, historically, done nothing to oppose—they then present a number of enticements to these parents, which portray a private market system as an avenue of exit from the failings of what they refer to as "a state monopoly."

One of the most compelling ways some voucher advocates advance their argument is by giving parents in poor neighborhoods the incorrect impression that a voucher will enable them to send their children to the kinds of private schools attended by the children of the affluent—"wealthy people have these choices . . . why, then, shouldn't you enjoy them too?"—even though they know that this enticing invitation is outrageously misleading. Vouchers equivalent to present levels of per-pupil spending in our urban schools would pay, at most, one quarter or one third of the tuition at the private schools attended by the privileged.

Another unconvincing argument made commonly by advocates for private markets—at least when they're speaking to poor people—is that schools receiving vouchers would be open in admissions policies to children of all economic levels and all levels of ability and would not favor children of the so-called "savvy" parents in a given neighborhood. This is a necessary claim for them to make in order to defuse the common charge that schools receiving vouchers will skim off the more successful children of more highly motivated parents, leaving the public schools with children who have greater problems and with parents who have fewer means to advocate on their behalf. The likelihood of selectivity in the admissions processes for private schools receiving vouchers is, for this reason, fervently denied.

But, as you and I know very well, even in the public system as it stands and even in schools in which there is no clear-cut selectivity, self-selectivity manages to do the job of guaranteeing that the children of the more effective parents are more likely to get into better schools than other children living in their neighborhood. In almost every case in which there is a limited number of high-rated public schools, it is the more aggressive and more knowledgeable parents who learn first about these schools and navigate the application process most successfully. By and large, these are the same parents who know how to get their children into Head Start programs in those neighborhoods where Head Start openings are very few, who are themselves among the better educated, or the better organized, among the parents of a poor community and are also the most likely to be welcomed, even courted, by a principal who struggles to attract the families that can bring a school stability and volunteer participation.

Even without a voucher system in existence in most states, the semi-private charter schools that exist in many cities typically claim that poverty levels for their students are no different from those of the students who attend the ordinary public schools in the same neighborhoods. They also insist that their admissions processes are nonselective, and they point, for instance, to a lottery approach that's often used to narrow down a large number of applicants. But when I asked the principal of one such school in the South Bronx how parents even knew enough to get into the lottery to start with, how they'd heard about the school and knew its application deadlines and the like, he said most of the parents "heard of us by word-of-mouth" or "read about us in newspaper stories." (There had been some favorable stories on the school in question in The New York Times, which could not fail to skew the field of applicants, since most people in the area were not readers of The Times, which is not widely sold in the South Bronx.)

I also noticed, when I visited the school, that I'd never been in any school in the South Bronx before that day in which so many kids were wearing new prescription glasses and had new attractive backpacks and appeared, in other ways, so well prepared for school—an exceptionality I've noticed in some of the other charter schools I've visited in other cities.

Reverend Martha Overall, the pastor of St. Ann's Church, who runs an afterschool program in the neighborhood in which my book Amazing Grace takes place, and where Pineapple and a number of her schoolmates used to spend a great deal of their time, has often made the observation that a seemingly transparent word like "poverty" can mask important differences in state of mind and frame of reference of specific parents in a poor community.

Even among parents who are very poor, as she has pointed out, there are distinctions of "connectedness," of "knowledgeability," of "elbow-pushing skills," that would never show up in the poverty statistics. Many of the parents of the children that she serves, she says, have never heard of any of the charter schools that episodically become the favorites of the press. If she mentions one of these schools, they give her "the same look they'd give me if I spoke of Andover or Groton."

Advocates for vouchers, nonetheless, tend to insist

that any difficulties represented by self-selectivity will cease to be real problems once the market mechanism of a voucher system and the "rational decision-making" they believe this will inevitably entail go into full effect. There is an element of almost blind faith in this supposition about rational decision-making that appears to brook no troubling intrusions from the real world in which children such as Pineapple and Ariel and Reginald and their parents actually dwell. One gets the sense that any evidence of uninformed and therefore damaging decision-making or, in the case of parents overwhelmed by problems in their private lives, the virtual absence of decision-making, is rejected by the privatizing advocates because it's incompatible with their beliefs or policy objectives or, one has to fear, forensic purposes.

One of the most influential voucher advocates, John Chubb, now a top executive at one of the private education corporations, goes so far as to take upon himself the mantle of defender of the poor against those who, like Reverend Overall, are in the trenches of the daily struggle on behalf of inner-city children and don't need to score points with their parents by romanticizing what they undergo. "It is really hard for me to believe," said Mr. Chubb in an interview he gave The New York Times, that if vouchers were available to parents of poor children, "those people couldn't decide on what they prefer." And he went still further in arguing that people who do not agree with him are being condescending to the poor by saying that poor parents are "too stupid" (Mr. Chubb's sarcastic words) to pick the schools they want their children to attend.

Mr. Chubb, like many voucher advocates, is an adept debater. But it's also possible he has no first-hand knowledge of how hard it is for many of the parents he refers to as "those people" to find out about such matters as a lottery for a specific private school or charter school, to make an appointment for an interview and receive a call-back from the school when an appointment is confirmed (large numbers of families I know in the South Bronx don't have working telephones), to get to the place they're supposed to go on the appointed day, and then to make a well-informed decision on the merits of the pedagogy that the school promotes.

Then, too, advocates for vouchers do not hesitate to contradict the claims they make in speaking to one audience when speaking to another. One of the disadvantages of public schools, says Mr. Chubb in a more candid statement than the one he made in speaking to The Times, is that they "must take whoever walks in the door" and "do not have the luxury of being able to select" their students. Under a voucher system, by comparison, "a constellation of . . . different schools serving different kinds of children differently would probably emerge." And in a book advancing private education markets, he makes the additional argument that schools "must be free to admit as many or as few students as they want, based on whatever criteria they think relevant—intelligence, interest, motivation, behavior, special needs. . . ."

The exercise of school choice, then, under a market system would belong only in small part to the parents of the poor. The ultimate choices would be made by those who own or operate a school. This is a rather different notion of school choice than the one most voucher advocates advance in seeking popular support, but it is only one of several contradictions in the arguments they make, depending on which portion of the population they are speaking to.

Frequently, for instance, in painting a scenario of schools that the recipients of vouchers might attend, advocates for vouchers point to Roman Catholic schools as instances of private institutions that might flourish in a system based on market competition, while they rarely speak of profit-driven schools run by a private corporation as potential beneficiaries of the system they propose. Instead, the idealistic motives that are commonly identified with inner-city Catholic schools are seized upon in order to position the discussion on an elevated ground of seemingly unselfish and high-minded goals.

Meanwhile, however, in writings narrowly directed at investors, all of these high-minded motives disappear and other benefits to be derived from vouchers suddenly emerge. This is where the gloves come off and any semblance of an altruistic purpose is replaced by practical considerations of a wholly different kind.

Some years ago, a friend of mine who worked on Wall Street handed me a stock market prospectus in which a group of analysts at an investment banking firm known as Montgomery Securities described the benefits that the privatizing of our public schools would offer to investors. "The education industry," according to these analysts, "represents, in our opinion, the final frontier of a number of sectors once under public control" that "have either voluntarily opened" or, they note in pointed terms, "been forced" to open up to private enterprise. Indeed, they write, "the education industry represents the largest market opportunity" since health care services were privatized during the 1970s.

Referring to private education companies as "EMOs" ("Education Management Organizations"), they note that college education offers some "attractive investment returns" for corporations too, but then return to what they see as the much greater profits to be gained by moving into public elementary and secondary schools. "The larger developing opportunity is in the K–12 EMO market, led by private elementary school providers," which, they emphasize, "are well positioned to exploit potential political reforms such as school vouchers. . . ."

Even now, without a widespread voucher system in effect, one of these analysts observes, private corporations are already "attracting outside capital" to launch or to expand their work in management of public schools. "The K–12 market," he continues in a phrase that may stir up your good satiric wrath a little more than usual, "is the Big Enchilada."

Language as predatory and outrightly cynical as this is never heard in the benign and civic-minded arguments that voucher advocates present when speaking to the parents of the poor. No references are made in these inducements to the likelihood that vouchers may unlock a new "frontier" for profit-making companies that have an appetite for big or little "enchiladas." Pineapple and Ariel and Dobie and Shaniqua would not likely have suspected that their little destinies, downgraded and diminished for so long by governmental penury, have suddenly become the object of so large an appetite.

Francesca, I know this next point is extremely delicate, but it troubles me that many Catholic educators do not seem to recognize that, by their support for vouchers, they are lending dignity to an idea that poses dangers which most thoughtful Catholic theologians with whom I've discussed this issue view with grave concern. I'm not thinking now exclusively about the profit-making corporations that would surely win the lion's share of public funds under the voucher system that the Catholic church supports. There is another and, I think, far greater danger here.

If vouchers can be used to underwrite a child's education at a school run by a Catholic church, they could obviously be used as well to underwrite enrollment at a private school run by another church, or mosque, or synagogue, including some religious groups that are infused with zealous and disturbing ideologies. There are also religiously affiliated schools that have been founded out of quietly or, in some cases, obviously racist motivations. I'm thinking, for example, of conservative white schools, often based in churches, modeled on the segregationist academies that came into existence in the South during the decade after *Brown* as sanctuaries for the children of white parents threatened by the prospect of race-mixing under programs of court-ordered integration. (It was these academies that first demanded "vouchers" by that name during the 1950s, an effort in which they were not successful but which leaves a precedent that voucher advocates today would like us to put out of mind.)

Ideology alone, entirely separate from religion, would undoubtedly inspire other interest groups— loyal followers of charismatic but invidious people such as David Duke, militant survivalists, people not particularly fond of Jews (or Catholics, for that matter)—to lay a claim to public subsidies for private education that advances their particular beliefs. Even the most abhorrent of these groups, moreover, might well make their entry into voucher markets through associated groups in local neighborhoods that may not look at first to be particularly toxic in their ideologies and which have the superficial trappings of respectability.

I wish that those among my friends who operate small Catholic schools, as well as some of the black activists in inner-city areas who look at vouchers as a way to offer an immediate escape-hatch to a small number of children from the problems of the public system as it stands, would think a little harder about "David Duke Academies," "Pat Robertson Academies," "Louis Farrakhan Academies," and the multitude of other pedagogic genies that will almost certainly climb out of the bottle of a tax-supported voucher system if it ever comes into widespread effect. They are making a Faustian bargain, and they ought to get to know the devil they are dealing with.

On rare occasions, voucher advocates concede that a degree of governmental supervision would be needed to prohibit schools identified with hateful ideologies from being the recipients of public funds. The problem here is that no instrument of supervision can control the many ways in which an ideology or bias is embedded in instruction. No matter what constraints are set in place, most Americans, I think, know very well what almost every teacher quickly learns and what you and I have talked about repeatedly: that education is not, and can never be, a wholly neutral enterprise.

Thus, even earnestly intended government restrictions upon doctrinal ingredients cannot control the dangerous degree to which the entries to an unrestricted voucher market will be able to affect the biases of children and the possibilities this holds for deepening divisions between groups already physically divided from each other and quite often fearful and distrustful of each other. We know how tenuous relationships already are between diverse groups in such racially divided cities as New York. How much more fragile might relationships between such groups become if we permit ourselves to concretize and deepen these divisions by the spawning of a multitude of ideologically, religiously, or ethnically established schools, supported by taxpayers?

A Massachusetts high school principal I've known for a long time told me that he still "can't actually figure out" how an idea like vouchers, long identified with interests of right-wing extremists and, historically, with the most flagrantly outspoken adversaries of school integration, has ended up today positioned so close to the center of respectable opinion.

One of the answers, I believe, is the painstaking labor that has been invested by the privatizing forces in advancing arguments that help to sanitize and rehabilitate the voucher concept by adhering strictly to the virtues they perceive in market competition, and, moreover, doing so in what are often very skillful writings that appear convincing to much of the mainstream media. Characteristic of these writings are a predilection for cool-headed exposition that conveys the seeming objectivity of academic social science, a tendency to simulate broad-mindedness by making reference, frequently respectful, to the work of liberals who disagree with them, and extensive pages of complex statistics that are not examined closely by most readers and, perhaps, not even meant to be examined, but which give these works the look of heft and substance one associates with scholarly production.

Frequently embedded in these even-tempered pages are incendiary passages in which the essence of the author's biases are stunningly displayed and crystallized. You mentioned this when you read The Bell Curve by Charles Murray, one of the most artful and, to give him credit, least evasive advocates for vouchers. In an earlier book that I don't think you've read, entitled Losing Ground, published in the 1980s, in which he makes his most extensive case for vouchers, Murray concedes without any hesitation that vouchers will not benefit all children equally. Some children, he writes, "whose parents do not play their part effectively," will end up in "bad schools" or "no schools at all." Others, who turn out to be least willing to be educated, will "drop by the wayside, failures of the system." Painful outcomes, unfortunate though they may be, are, he believes, the "natural results" when people are obliged to make responsible decisions and the government does not try to compensate for their mistakes. "Some people are better than others," he concludes. "They deserve more of society's rewards."

It is these bright and gleaming gems of brutal ideology that energize the writings of a number of the advocates for vouchers and lend them the mystique of being unafraid to think unthinkable ideas or speak unspeakable beliefs. But, shocking as they are, these controversial passages are rapidly absorbed into a larger fabric of apparent intellectual substantiality.

It is a tribute to the real success that voucher advocates have had in publicizing their beliefs that I'm hearing many of the less incendiary arguments they make from friends and neighbors even here in relatively isolated northern Massachusetts: people, for the most part, who are neither very rich nor very poor but want to send their children to an independent school and suddenly are asking why they cannot get some money from the government to pay for it. Is it fair, they ask essentially, that they have to "pay for education twice," once in the tuition costs for private school, and once in taxes to support a public system they do not intend to use? If their kids don't go to public school, according to this thinking, why don't they deserve to get part of their taxes back to pay for the tuition at the schools their children do attend?

This seemingly quite innocent request is what I call "The Voucher Question" in its purest form. If education is perceived not as a universal good but as a personal commodity, and nothing more, to be consumed for personal advantage only—if this is *all* it is—then it's very hard to argue with a parent who sincerely thinks she's being double-billed.

One of the parents who has posed this argument to me is a middle class white woman who lives not too far from me in one of the smaller cities in this part of Massachusetts and who sends her daughter to a

Christian school. (Quite a number of these schools are popping up around the country, and no longer only in the South.) She's a religious woman, dedicated to her daughter and her church, socially conservative, likable in many ways, but very tough and hard-nosed in this one respect: She sees her daughter's education in exactly the same way she thinks of any other item that she pays for, like a car or suit of clothes, except she knows that education's more important. She buys a car. She buys her child a dress. She buys a year in school. She doesn't have to buy a second dress for someone else's child. Why, then, does she have to buy "a second education," which is how it seems to her, for a child who attends the public school her daughter used to go to?

How do you answer someone like this woman, who grew up in the 1980s in the business-minded Bush and Reagan years and sees the world in almost wholly mercantile and individual and private terms?

I suppose I could try to make the argument, because she *is* religious, that her support of public schools—without diminishing the funding of those schools by seeking a tax credit or a voucher of some sort—would be in keeping with her Christian principles and with her sense of obligation to the poorer children living in her city, which has seen a recent increase in Hispanic and black and Laotian children, who rely almost entirely on the public system. But even though I know she makes her offerings at church to help the shelters and soup kitchens that some of the recent immigrants depend on, it is clear that she would not extend this sense of obligation to the point of underwriting public education for the children of poor people if she were not forced to do so by taxation.

The point I wish that I could make to her is this: In paying taxes for the sustenance of public schools, we're not just buying something for ourselves. We're buying something for the benefit of the community in which we live, and for the state and, ultimately, for the nation. In other words, I wish that I could speak to her of public schools, with all the serious challenges they face and all of the inequities they bear, as instruments of an intended decency—a decency that is, admittedly, not realized now in many sectors of the public system as it stands but one that generations of Americans have ardently believed, and most believe today, to be worth striving for. The trouble is that, growing up during the years she did, and having the beliefs that she now holds, she no longer thinks of public schools that way, and many people in her situation don't.

Francesca, it's not easy for me to concede this, but I think the gradual tilt in public attitudes about the privatizing movement is the fault, to some degree, of those of us who do support the public schools but have, in recent years at least, done so rather cringingly, almost apologetically, and without presenting a compelling vision of our own. Some of us have wasted too much time in what I'd call "defensive nibbling" and tiresome nitpicking at statistics that the voucher advocates often put forth. I think, for instance, that we've squandered too much energy in trying to discredit what they claim to be the higher levels of achievement of the students in at least some of the private schools or hybrid schools that they support, which I believe are often indisputable, given the selectivity and self-selectivity we have observed.

My own beliefs about this are not always welcome among leftist intellectuals, who are often burdened by a cavalier hostility not just to organized religion but to religious faith of any kind at all. Still, I think there is a place in this debate for matters that are frankly spiritual, and even theological.

Many people in the Christian schools who speak in gospel language obviously do not arrange admissions to their schools by the example of the gospels or the mandates of Judeo-Christian principles. If they did, they wouldn't turn their backs on children who do not have parents who can fight for them aggressively and skillfully. I don't think we ought to let the propagandists of the right expropriate our testaments as freely as they do. The Hebrew prophets and the followers of Jesus did not make a false god out of elbow-pushing skills and hard-nosed competition. "Savviness" was not their ministry. We ought to remind Americans of that.

In other words, I think we should, at least in part, be making a religious argument against a movement that religious people frequently support. A political agenda that attempts to reconcile Social Darwinism, market competition, an overt appeal to separatist crusaders, and covert appeals to subtle bigots of all racial groups is simply not compatible with the religious, theological, and moral underpinnings of American society. The mainstream churches—which, with the exception of the Roman Catholic Church, largely share my feelings on this matter—ought to be speaking out on this more boldly than they do.

But so too should our teachers. Some of the novice teachers I've been meeting seem to have only the vaguest knowledge of the forces that are now arrayed against them. They note with disapproval that scarce funds, so badly needed in the classroom, are increasingly diverted, under mandates of No Child Left Behind, to hire profit-making corporations to conduct test-preparation sessions in their buildings. Some also note that many charter schools and growing numbers of the inner-city public schools are being run by private corporations, which they also view uneasily. But few of the teachers who observe these trends see them, as they need to see them, as the first steps in a long, well-orchestrated, and well-financed plan to privatize the public education sector altogether.

Nor do these teachers seem to recognize that the inevitable end point of these strategies, if they succeed, will be a sweeping transformation of the very nature of their own profession, by which the teacher's role will cease to be a "calling" as they think of it today and will be instead that of a worker in "an enterprise" in which their students will no longer be regarded as "the kids we teach" and intimately know and usually come to love but will instead become our "clients" or our "customers."

I told you once, Francesca, that I made the brief mistake of toying with the privatizing notion when I was about your age and thought myself to be a lot more clever than I really was, but quickly recognized the damage this would do by shifting the focus of attention and commitment from the collectivity of struggle in the public system to the interests of a group of individuals whose children were at least a little better off, both socially and psychologically, than most of the thousands of poor children we would leave behind.

I have atoned for that mistake during the decades since. You, Francesca, happily have nothing to atone for. In this respect, as in a number of others, you have been by your example a much better role model to me than I have been to you. I know you are too generous to say this, or to think this, but I happen to believe it's true.

CHAPTER TWELVE

It Is Evil to Tell Lies
to Children

Dear Francesca,

Thank you for sending me the Yevtushenko poem. "Telling lies to the young is wrong. Proving to them that lies are true is wrong." I liked especially the final words: "Forgive no error you recognize. It will repeat itself, increase, and afterwards our pupils will not forgive in us what we forgave."

It naturally reminds me of our talks about "diversity" instruction and the injury it does to children when we either tell them things we know to be untrue or simply offer them materials we know to be misleading and then stand back and allow the lies to sink in quietly.

About ten years ago, an author named James Loewen wrote a book entitled Lies My Teacher Told Me. I'm told that an updated version of this book is in the works. If so, it is badly needed now, because the same deceptions, many of them in social studies textbooks, are purveyed to children still, while a newer body of deceptions, many far more subtle and insidious, have proliferated since.

One of the standard themes in social studies lessons, for example, that has remained pretty much unaltered since I was a boy is the reassuring notion that, if great injustices exist, our nation's mode of governance provides an avenue of redress through the legal process. An individual or, in the instance I am going to describe, a group of individuals who believe they are unfairly treated may, according to this notion, place their faith in legal action which, if it's victorious, will lead to transformation of conditions they believe to be intolerable.

It is not this notion in itself so much as the simplistic way that it's presented, with no parallel reference to the frequency with which a legal judgment is obstructed and invalidated by political maneuvers on the part of legislators and executives, that leaves our students, when they later understand the way the system really works, with a crushing sense of their own impotence as citizens.

This issue is directly relevant to children in our inner-city schools because at this moment, as you know, there are legal actions challenging the inequalities in funding for our public schools in the courts of several states, some of which began as long as 30 years ago. In repeated instances, after years of litigation, these suits have been successful and the local media have heralded the imminence of "a whole new order" of equality and justice for the children of the poor. But, with very few exceptions, the students who are plaintiffs in these cases never see the benefits that legal victories have led them to expect, because political forces in their states brazenly defy court orders and, moreover, do so with impunity.

In Ohio, for example, more than a decade after a suit was filed in the early 1990s on behalf of children in low-income districts, the state's supreme court had determined three times that the system of school finance was in violation of the constitution of the state, yet the governor and legislature thumbed their noses at these rulings and were never forced to face contempt citations. A black teenager in Columbus or Toledo who defied a ruling of the court would likely find himself in prison. No such punishment is visited upon a governor who does the same.

Again, in New York, a similar suit, filed initially in 1993 on behalf of New York City's children, was not decided for ten years and, even then, the court allowed the governor and legislative branch an extra year to remedy the inequalities it had excoriated in an eloquent decision. A year later, in 2003, after the state had failed to act, New York's highest court affirmed the trial court's decision and issued another deadline for compliance by 2004, which the state again refused to meet and which the governor appealed. Finally, in 2006, after yet another round of litigation and delay, a newly constituted court, its political makeup altered by two new appointees of the governor, essentially removed the legal branch of government from further action in the case, leaving corrective measures to be taken by those same executive and legislative branches that had underfunded New York City's children, by this point, for decades.

Even if a more enlightened New York governor and legislative body should at long last act upon the constitutional requirements the state has disobeyed for all these years, this can never compensate those students who were little children when this case was filed but are little kids no more. Courts do not grant children reparations for the loss of childhood.

New York City teachers often talk with me about the state's obstruction of these legal judgments and the toll that this has taken on the schools in which they teach. Why not talk about it also with their students? It certainly would pump new life into those usually very boring and perfunctory discussions of "the three branches of government" if teachers were to bring news clippings and additional materials about this story into class in order to provide their students with a vivid opportunity to explore a concept that is now presented with a fatal incompleteness in the texts provided to them by the very state that is shortchanging them.

Francesca, I know very well that lessons like the one that I'm proposing are unlikely to be suited to the children in the early elementary grades—among other reasons, because so much reading matter would be needed to present these issues in their full complexity. I'm also not suggesting that the teachers in a middle school or high school ought to set out in a mindless and destructive way to undermine their students' faith in the ideals that underlie American democracy. But I think we have an obligation to empower those we teach to understand that this democracy is very much a work in progress and that if they can't achieve the skills to take an active role as citizens in struggles to *bring* progress in their grown-up years, the injustices they suffer now will never change.

Many teachers tell me of the strategies they use to introduce these kinds of lessons but avoid the risk of dominating the opinions of their students by the force of their own arguments. One of these strategies—but one, admittedly, that calls for a great deal of preparation on the part of teachers—is to create a package of historical materials, contemporary journalistic writings, tapings of strong editorial opinions offered on TV, as well as transcripts of court hearings and the like, and to construct from these materials a set of lesson plans that can engage their students in examination and analysis of certain of the more familiar textbook verities and also enable them to compare these verities with the evidence of their experience.

In one illuminating recent case in Florida, for instance, the voters passed a constitutional amendment to require a reduction in the size of classes in the public schools. The Florida governor at the time, Jeb Bush, who was an advocate for vouchers and high-stakes exams but who opposed the class-size measure, announced in advance at a meeting of his legislative allies at which a reporter happened to be present, "I have a couple of devious plans" to resist the decision of the voters if the amendment should be passed. After its passage, the governor and legislature made it clear that they would not obey the new amendment, even though it now was part of the state's constitution.

"Since 2002," according to a story in The Palm Beach Post, Republican leaders had insisted that obeying the amendment was going to "cost too much money" and therefore refused to allocate the funds for school construction that would meet the terms of the amendment. A few years later, "flush with extra billions of dollars in tax revenue," the paper said, the same Republican leaders have come up with "a new reason" to defy the law: "There is now not enough time to build the necessary schools by the required deadlines."

As a result, according to The Post, Republican leaders introduced bills in both houses of the legislature to *increase* the size of classes and to permit "two or more classes" to be forced to "share a single room." Legislators who believed the children of the state had been betrayed by the behavior of the governor and legislature were reluctant to bring legal action to compel them to obey the constitution, because of the power of the governor. "Suing and angering a group of . . . lawmakers is one thing," said The Post. "Suing and enraging . . . the brother of the president of the United States is another."

In the end, the legislature came up with a half-hearted solution. "Class size" was redefined, at least for now, to mean the student-teacher *ratio* in any given room, rather than the total number of students in that room, which permitted schools to double or triple the number of teachers in a room, then pack in as many children as the fire codes allowed. Meanwhile, the legislators allocated only a small fraction of the money that economists have estimated it will take to build enough new schools to permit authentic class reduction in the sense in which most people understand that term.

If you were a sixth or eighth grade teacher in the state of Florida, Francesca, I can imagine how you'd sink your teeth into this story, which would represent an ideal opportunity to let your students judge the merits of the arguments and the morality of their elected leaders. If you were to try to do a project like this with a class of students, you would probably need to give them documentation also of the great extremes of class size found in various school districts, so that they would have a chance to understand that classrooms holding 32 or 35 or 40 children, which are common in the upper grades of inner-city schools in many states and are legally permitted now in Florida, are not the norm in the United States, are not inevitable or universal or God-given or, as poor kids often come to think, "the way it's simply supposed to be," "the way it is for everyone."

It might be fair, as well, to cite those who insist

that class size is irrelevant to the success of students, although, if we do this, it would be instructive to our students to investigate the size of classes at the schools to which such people send *their* children.

In wealthy districts, in which those who shape our nation's policies most commonly reside, I typically walk into a first or second grade with no more than 16 or 18 children in the room, and into high school classes with no more than 20. At the exclusive private schools here in New England, such as Andover and Exeter, classes are commonly limited to 12 or 15 students at the most. President Bush, as you know, went to Andover, as did his brother and his father. If very small class size, and the individual attention this permits each student to receive, is good for the son of a president or for the daughter of an influential business CEO, I think students might conclude that it's every bit as good for the poorest child of the poorest woman in Miami.

Am I proposing that a teacher in Miami ought to stand in class and launch an angry and one-sided onslaught on the governor or legislature of the state? Certainly not. In order to be even-handed in the presentation of such issues, teachers need to find a way to give their students oppositional materials so that they will have a genuine, not token, opportunity to derive their own conclusions. At the same time, I don't think teachers should attempt to hide their own beliefs and, as you and I discussed, it's probably impossible to do so. Rather, I think they ought to be transparent in defining these *as* their beliefs so that their kids can judge or challenge what they say accordingly.

The most common result that I encounter when I make my own position clear in a discussion of a controversial matter with a class of children is much like the one that I described at the Martin Luther King School in New York, in which there was a division of the house within the class, with students taking starkly opposite positions and with several of those students standing up for their beliefs with healthy energy and intellectual intensity. Classes like these are never dull. Wherever the majority of kids end up in these debates, they are at very least provoked to dig out of the usual passivity that leads so many inner-city high school kids to slump down in their chairs, hoods pulled up around their heads, and simply drop out of participation altogether.

I never feel affronted when a student or a group of students who do not agree with me become so animated that their comments to me verge on impoliteness. (Teenage kids, as you know well from your experience in high school, are very good at put-downs, whether with a shrug, a cutting word or two, or by the skillful uses of sarcasm.) I love it when this happens. I revel in their oppositional mentalities. I know for sure that they're not bored, or acquiescent, and that they are actually *thinking*.

Francesca, I'm aware that once again I'm going on a bit too long, so I'll try to be as brief as possible in speaking of a few last instances of what I think are coming to be dangerous deceptions, or at least deceptions by omission, of the students in too many of our schools.

One of these is what I call "The Hortatory Lie," which gives the children in some of the worst, most poorly funded, and most hypersegregated public schools the relentless message that success or failure in their academic work is a matter wholly of their own self-will, their own determination, their own perseverance, and that the external world—the governor, the school board, the determination of the white society to keep them at a distance where they can't contaminate the education of the middle class—has no role at all in preventing them from learning.

In Seattle, for example, in a segregated school that bore the name of Thurgood Marshall, the principal had taken pains to make it very difficult for kids to learn who Thurgood Marshall was or what it is that makes him an important moral figure in our history. The principal's reasoning, as I surmised, was that an honest recognition of the work of Justice Marshall in attempting to abolish racial segregation would have caused an undercurrent of persistent irony within a school that represented almost everything that Marshall had regarded as abhorrent.

Instead of presenting Marshall as the lifelong warrior for justice that he was, therefore, the principal had altered his persona to that of some sort of middle-level corporate employee who exemplified the virtues of obedience to rules and regulations, good managerial abilities, self-discipline, and oldfashioned bootstrap values of self-help.

"I will listen and I will follow directions," according to the Thurgood Marshall Pledge that was posted in the school and which the children were encouraged to recite repeatedly. "If it is to be, it's up to me," the poster said. Other chants and slogans like this were embedded in the school's daily activities. At a morning assembly I attended on my second visit to the school, the entire student body stood and chanted, "I have confidence that I can learn," exactly 30 times.

At this school, as at innumerable inner-city schools, these chantings were accompanied by rhythmic clapping of the hands or snapping of the fingers or by stamping on the floor. To the extent that some of the students really do get into this, it can be a lively and invigorating way to start the day. At the same time, politically conservative white people visiting these schools often seem to be almost too gratified to hear black and Hispanic children speaking in these terms. If it's up to "them," the message seems to be, it isn't up to "us," which appears to sweep the deck of many possibly expensive obligations we may otherwise believe our nation needs to contemplate.

And, to say this in the bluntest words, Francesca, when we ask these children to repeat in unison that "if it is to be, it's up to me," we are asking them to say something which, while they have no way of knowing this, is simply not the truth. Does the education system have no role in what this child is to be? Do taxpayers have no role in this? Do Congress and the courts and local legislators have no role in setting up the possibilities of what is "to be," or not to be, within these children's opportunities to learn? Why are the debates about state distribution of resources for our schools so heated, and the opposition to a fairer distribution on the part of wealthy districts so intense, if citizens do not believe that fiscal policies enacted by the government have a decisive role in the determination of the destinies of children?

Some people argue that these chanting rituals function as a useful form of therapy for students who come to these schools already badly damaged by conditions in their neighborhoods or by the legacy of history. Still, autohypnosis is no substitute for the provision of resources, the small size of classes, or the pleasantness of the environment within a school that other students in the greener places of our nation take as their entitlement as children of a very rich democracy.

The hortatory lie, however, is a necessary subset of what I would call "The Ultimate Lie" presented to the children in our poorest public schools. This is the lie of equal opportunity, which is still presented in the textbooks with the same unwavering tenacity as it was done when I was a child. It is a myth that flies in the face of so much common knowledge that it is remarkable that text materials continue to adhere to it.

When Pineapple was in fifth grade in the South Bronx, to give an obvious example, she received, in annual per-pupil spending, only about $11,500 for her education, while children in the nearby town of Bronx-ville (99 percent white, 1 percent black and Hispanic), a mere 20-minute ride by car from Pineapple's front door, were receiving almost $19,000 and children in the wealthy suburb of Manhasset, where some of the children and grandchildren of my Harvard classmates go to school, were receiving more than $22,000. In the same year, high school students in Chicago and in all-black East St. Louis in the southern part of Illinois were receiving less than half of what was spent on chil-dren at such well-known schools as Highland Park and Deerfield High, serving wealthy suburbs of Chicago. Similar extremes of inequality continue to exist in al-most every section of the nation.

Children who are being shortchanged by their government have the right to know enough about this to assess the myth of equal opportunity that is pur-veyed to them. Paradoxically, the kids who go to the most richly funded schools learn a great deal more about these inequalities, usually in classes that exam-ine U.S. social history, than almost any inner-city chil-dren do. The reason I know this is that several of my books, particularly Savage Inequalities, have been adopted for the upper-level classes at such first-rate institutions as New Trier High, which I learn when students at these schools send me the term papers they have written or when they sometimes even call me on the phone to ask for interviews while they are writing them. Thus, the kids who benefit directly from injustice learn much more about it than the ones who are its victims.

So long as myths and misconceptions about equal education remain unexamined in the schools that serve the poor, these kids are left to wrestle with the crippling belief that their repeated failings in comparison with affluent white children are entirely the result of an inherent defect in their character or cultural inheritance, a lack of will, a lack of basic drive and normal aspiration, or, as many have no choice but to believe, a deficit in their intelligence.

Teachers working in these schools need to find a way to deal with this directly. If handled with great sensitivity, a classroom project that makes clear the formidable odds that are aligned against these students does not crush their confidence but, much to the reverse, it stiffens their resolve and stirs an adversarial intensity. It grants the kids a steeling of the will to fight these odds not only by the hard work that they do in school but also by developing a sense of future potency to act within political arenas, not unlike the sense of moral potency young people of their age were bold enough to act upon some 50 years ago and which, from small beginnings, grew into a force that shook the conscience of American society.

A final lie that's being propagated widely to our inner-city students—or, maybe better stated, an attractively presented package of misleading expectations—is directly tied to those I've just described. This is the notion, spreading like a pedagogic wildfire through administrative circles in our urban schools right now, that students, starting at about the age of ten when they apply to middle school, or else at age thirteen when they apply to high school, ought to be induced to set their sights not on the open-ended and unlimited objectives for their academic futures you and I enjoyed but instead upon specific choices of careers.

The great deception here is that most children rarely have the slightest way to know, when they are ten, thirteen, or even sixteen years of age, what choices actually exist in life in terms of work, in terms of future intellectual activity, in terms of the full range of aspirations and rewards that are available in our society, or know their own hearts well enough to be prepared to choose.

I didn't know when I was ten years old what I'd like to do in life. I doubt that you did either. I didn't even have a good idea of this when I was seventeen. I didn't know enough about *myself* to have arrived at a decision of so much importance. Nor did I know about a broad enough array of options to determine which of them might satisfy the mix of goals or even halfway realistic dreams that fill the minds of most young people of that age. The "choice of a career" demanded of a student who is just beginning adolescence, or is in the midst of adolescence, means close to zero if that student has no way to know what choices he or she may actually have.

In spite of this reality, school systems in the

urban core are busily setting up what are described as "industry-embedded" schools or, in a slightly more sophisticated form, "career-identified academies," for which children are supposed to choose during their final year of elementary school or, depending on the state or district, in the final year of middle school. Although the choices offered in some of these theme-based schools now and then sound modestly egalitarian, and sometimes rather challenging, at least in the names they're given or in their promotional brochures, many of them are frankly aimed at getting kids who are not viewed as future college candidates, and certainly not viewed as cultural contributors to our society, to settle for "more realistic goals" that are regarded as appropriate for children of their economic class and racial origins.

Several cities, for example, operate career academies where black and Hispanic students are provided training in the so-called "health professions," which does not mean that many of these children are provided with the preparation to go on to universities and become our future cardiologists or surgeons but that most are being readied for the lower-level, less remunerative job-slots in our hospitals and nursing homes. In other cities, there are schools that channel black and Hispanic students into hotel work and cooking. In Los Angeles, at all-black and Hispanic Fremont High, students who were fully capable of higher education and who poured their hearts out to me when I spent two hours in their class, were being steered instead to classes that prepared them for the garment industry.

If industry-embedded schools or programs such as these were ever seriously proposed for children in suburban areas like Brookline, Lexington, or Concord, Massachusetts, or Glencoe and Winnetka, or Manhasset, or Grosse Point, I think we know, Francesca, how the parents would react. A superintendent who came up with this suggestion might quickly find himself without a job. No matter what high-minded rhetoric is used by those in school-and-business partnerships who are promoting these career academies for children of minorities, they are confections of apartheid that would be rejected out of hand in schools that serve the privileged.

Inevitably, in a nation with as many schools and districts as we have in the United States, there are bound to be some notable exceptions to the pattern I've described. A number of altruistic groups in the nonprofit sector have managed to create career academies in which career objectives have been wedded to authentic academic preparation and where the emphasis on "readiness for work" does not automatically exclude the courses needed for pre-college preparation. But these *are* exceptions and I have to tell you truthfully, Francesca, that too frequently the "academic" and "pre-college" emphasis within these kinds of schools is more a matter of the optimistic claims presented by school systems than that of the actual experience of students who end up enrolled within these institutions. I read many lofty-sounding and expensively produced materials distributed by school boards or by groups that sponsor schools like these; but when I visit many of these schools, what I see before my eyes are terminal academies.

In spite of the exceptions, which receive the largest share of media attention since they offer opportunities for upbeat stories ("Hope within the Ashes," as the headlines tend to go), the overall pattern of reductionist instruction for black and Hispanic children represents the restoration of a practice that has not been seen on such a widespread scale since the era of those training schools that were familiar substitutes for academic high schools for black students in the southern states during the years before the *Brown* decision. The actual name that was given to those schools, as Congressman John Lewis recently reminded me, was "training schools for coloreds." Although their students did sometimes receive an academic education, they were far more commonly prepared for the subordinate positions which, he said, were deemed to be most fitting for young people of their race. As segregation has returned to U.S. education, he observed, so too have new versions of the institutions by which it has been historically accompanied.

Most students who attend these schools today will never know, until it's far too late, that what they're being given is a stripped-down course of training that will narrow their potential options rather than a course of education that will widen them. Children who are being channeled into what is nothing less than a diminished intellectual existence and diminished status in the economic order, solely on the basis of the color of their skin, need to be alerted early to the fate that school officials have in store for them.

A tough analysis of what "careerist training" actually implies ought to be a straight-out and substantial portion of an elementary school's fifth grade curriculum. If it is not, teachers need to find a way to make it so, no matter what the criticism they incur. Yevtushenko's warning that our pupils will not forgive in us "what we forgave" ought to represent a solemn invocation to those who have forged a bond of loyalty with children they have known during their years of innocence and to whom they owe the unabated honesty that loyalty demands.

Your little kids, Francesca, have not learned the uses of those big-time lies that textbooks tell and many leaders of our urban districts seem to feel obliged to propagate. They do tell fibs, and I have noticed in your class that, when they do, they usually adhere to them quite stubbornly.

I still remember the day when you saw something that you said looked like "white powder" falling on the floor from one of Dobie's pockets and you questioned him about this and he said that there was "no white powder" in his pocket. Even when you pointed to the powder on the floor and scooped some up and held it right in front of him, he just stared you in the face and still insisted that it wasn't "no white powder."

You said, if I remember right, that you finally stuck your hand into his pocket and were quite amazed to find that it was packed with sugar! When you asked him why he was collecting sugar, you said he confessed to you that he liked sugar with his Cheerios and had gotten worried that it might soon go out of supply. So every time he saw a sugar bowl at home or in a neighbor's house he'd grab some sugar in his hand and put it in his pocket, where he had apparently been saving it for quite a while. Even at that point, though, he still stuck to his guns. You said he told you once again it wasn't "no white powder," which I guess was technically correct.

"That child is too smart for me," you said.

Still, the fibs your children tell, although they sometimes cause a flurry of brief tears for someone in the class whom they have fibbed against, are light-years from the kinds of all-consuming lies that cut into the very hearts of children in so many of our inner-city schools and, by omission or intention, amputate their capability to understand the world in which they someday must prevail, shriveling their destinies.

Thank you, dear Francesca, for sending me this poem of Yevtushenko.

CHAPTER THIRTEEN

Loss of Innocence

*More Reflections on the Middle
Schools and High Schools*

Dear Francesca,

I'm glad you prompted me to say a little more about the secondary years. I know you look ahead and worry what will happen to your children when it's time for them to move on, just five years from now, to middle schools, and then to high schools, where they will no longer be protected by the warm and safe environment your principal has managed to create for them.

"Innocent little girls," you wrote, "seem to lose that innocence with a heart-breaking frequency once they leave their elementary schools." Little boys whose whimsical behavior or defiant postures—"even if they drive us crazy every other day," you said—still seem adorable to us when they are six or eight years old, "do not always seem so lovable to teachers in a middle school" who have to cope with them when they're twelve or thirteen.

This is one reason why I was opposed to middle schools, right from the start, when they began replacing junior high schools in the early 1970s. I thought that keeping students with us in the grade schools for one extra year, especially the female students, helped us to protect them from the multiple enticements that are present in a school where some of the boys, if they've repeated grades, may be 15 already.

Indeed, if any school administrator were to ask for my opinion now, I'd suggest we do away with middle schools entirely. Instead, I'd argue for incorporating all three years of middle school into an upper level of the elementary school, so that we'd be able to exploit the attachments we have formed with children since they were in kindergarten or in first or second grade as barriers against that early loss of innocence that you described.

In the K-through-8 schools I envision, older children, even though their academic work would be at secondary levels, would be given opportunities to serve as mentors and "team leaders" to the younger children in the building. Scheduling arrangements might be made to enable some of them to spend a portion of their schoolday working as "assistant teachers" in the classrooms of the early grades, reading with children, helping them with basic math, and, by so doing, reinforcing their own competence in both those areas, which, I've always been convinced, is one of the best ways older students can perfect their own grasp of those elemental skills.

The very mature girl in the fifth grade at your school who spends as much time in your classroom as her teacher will allow has obviously learned a lot from working at your side, especially in her writing skills, to which, I notice, you devote considerable time when she stays there with you after class. But it also seems that she's acquired qualities of serious responsibility and generosity in tending to the little ones, which have had a gentling effect upon her temperament.

Sooner or later, though, as things stand now in most urban districts, these youngsters will leave elementary school when they're ten or eleven years old and will enter middle school a few months later. Whether in their middle schools or later in their high school years, the majority of students who don't qualify for the selective schools to which admissions are determined by exams are going to find themselves in settings that are likely to be even more demoralizing and more overcrowded than the one in which Pineapple found herself when she attended elementary school.

Once, when she was in fourth grade, Pineapple described the basement cafeteria at P.S. 65 as "Lunchroom Hell." When I went down there with her for her lunch, I didn't think her words were overstated in the least. Unhappily, it's usually no better and often it's a good deal worse down in the basement lunchrooms of the middle schools and high schools that await these kids a few years later on.

At one high school in New York (3,600 students in a school that's legally suited for no more than 1,800), a group of ninth grade boys and girls whose classes I was visiting asked me to come down with them for lunch one day. Principals sometimes grow alarmed when I accede to these requests. ("Oh no!" one principal in another city told me when two of her students said that they were taking me downstairs for lunch. "We have a lovely catered lunch arranged here in my office." "Un-uh!" one of the students said. The principal reluctantly allowed me to go downstairs with the students.)

In this instance in New York, because of the intensive overcrowding of the school, lunch was served in a series of shifts, the first of which began around nine-thirty, with the final shift a little after two. The kids who had lunch in the first shift didn't eat much, because they were not yet hungry, but grew ravenous by noon. Some of them, I was told, got so hungry by the middle of the day that they'd simply leave the school, illegally, to buy lunch somewhere else and usually would not come back.

Happily, the kids who took me down to lunch were on a mid-day shift. But the atmosphere was still chaotic and we had to wait for nearly 20 minutes before we could get in line, and even once we'd gotten into line, the line moved very slowly. Almost inevitably, fights broke out. A group of students who had not yet been allowed to get in line and were waiting at their table got into a fight so violent that a security officer was called and had to intervene before a boy who had been slammed down on the table could be injured badly by a group of angry boys who stood around him. The students who had taken me in charge just shrugged at this, because it was so commonplace.

Visitors from outside these neighborhoods who witness confrontations like this often make the unkind observation that "these students act like animals." But if you treat these kids like animals, herding them along for squalid feedings like so many cattle rather than providing them with even minimal civility, it's not surprising to me that they act accordingly.

It isn't just the kids, moreover, who become degraded under these conditions. Teachers and lunch monitors who are perfectly good-natured people in most other situations cease to be their normal selves when they are put into these settings, shouting orders at the students, uttering harsh imprecations, forfeiting their customary dignity in their frenzied efforts to control the chaos in which they become engulfed and which they often worsen by their own behavior.

Even the man who was in charge of serving food, in this case, lost his sense of self-control and turned into a kind of monster when the kids who were escorting me got up to the front part of the line. A ninth grade student who was just in front of me asked me what I'd like to have for lunch. I was feeling weak by then because I have a problem with blood sugar and begin to tremble when I haven't eaten for a while. I told her that I'd like a sandwich and some chocolate milk, if they happened to have chocolate milk that day. She peered ahead so she could see the counter, and she said they did.

But when we finally got up to the counter and she chose my food for me, the burly red-faced man behind the counter took my tray out of my hands and said I couldn't eat. "Why not?" the student asked. He said it was because I didn't have some kind of card that was required for I.D. A teacher who was watching this told him that I was a guest, but he had grown enraged by now and wouldn't let go of the tray. The teacher grabbed the tray with both her hands and tried to take it from him. The two of them were literally wrestling with that tray of food while the students who were with me grew embarrassed that I had to witness this.

As it turned out, I never got my food. But the spunky ninth grade girl who had decided that it was her job to do the best she could for me grabbed a container of chocolate milk and slipped it in my pocket while the man behind the counter argued with the teacher. I was grateful for her larceny.

Often, when I'm in one of these "uglifying" schools (that's a word that Gwendolyn Brooks once used in writing to me, which she counterposed to "happifying" situations), I am reminded of the very different atmosphere I find at high schools almost anywhere I go outside these areas of concentrated poverty, not only in the wealthiest communities but also in the schools that serve the mainstream of our student population. The lunchrooms themselves are generally pleasant places. At a high school in New Hampshire recently, I watched the students sitting at small tables shaped in different geometric forms that had tiled surfaces with Mexican designs. In good weather they could eat outside at tables on a terraced area that adjoined the lunchroom. In some of the nicest schools students can select their food from salad bars, with all the usual amenities, like bacon bits and large black olives and raw carrots, that you'd see in lunchrooms at expensive colleges.

The students chat, or work together on their homework, while they have their lunch. Teachers stop by to sit with them sometimes. It's all relaxed, and comfortable, and calm. Nobody looking at these kids would say they "act like animals."

Here's why I've gone on about this for so long: I believe aesthetics count a great deal in the education of our children. Beautiful surroundings refine the souls of children. Ugly surroundings coarsen their mentalities. It's one of the most decisive ways by which we draw the line of caste and class between two very different sectors of our student populations.

Sometimes, Francesca, when I'm saying things like this to you, I stop and smile at myself because I know that when I start to grow incensed about a matter like aesthetics in our public schools, I'm preaching to the choir. I already know, because I've seen the world that you've created for the children in your class, that you value the importance of the physical surroundings every bit as much as I do. But it's harder to create these islands of serenity and beauty in the inner-city high schools, where the very walls and corridors, covered often with graffiti, and the stench that comes from bathroom doorways shape the school environment as much as any single classroom does. And the classrooms of a high school are not "home" to children in the way that elementary classrooms are, since students move continually from class to class. So even the efforts that a teacher makes to liven up the walls and chalkboards of the room where he or she routinely works are countermanded by the sights and smells the kids encounter all day long, before they come into that room and after they leave it.

I've also been in high schools where, because of overcrowding, many students do not even have real classrooms. They go to class, instead, in what the schools call "portables," which is, as you know, a fancy term for trailers. At one high school in Los Angeles that had an enrollment of 5,000 students when I visited two years ago, more than a third of the classes took place in these trailers, many of which were stacked beside each other in what once had been a recreation area.

For some reason, they don't call these tawdry structures "trailers" in Los Angeles; nor do they call them "portables." Instead, they call them "bungalows."

But they don't *look* like bungalows! I can assure you, if you're ever in Los Angeles and go to visit classes in some of these trailers, "bungalow" will be the last word that will come into your mind. Because of the role they fill in packing in the surplus children of minorities in California, I call them "containables," an expression which, of course, offends my white friends in the school administration there.

Teachers I know in Los Angeles, however, do not cringe when I use terms like that. Many who work at dreadful schools like Fremont High and Theodore Roosevelt High use even stronger language to convey their anger at the sordid atmosphere they and their students are expected to endure without complaint. These teachers spend their whole lives working in environments in which not one of their perennial critics in the business sector of Los Angeles would likely agree to work a single day.

As you know, Francesca, one of the most commonly proposed solutions to the problems of the high schools I've been visiting is to subdivide them into smaller schools, or "mini-schools," housed in the same building or, if the funding is available, in separate buildings of their own. Usually, school systems can't afford to place these schools in separate buildings, so the children in the small schools share the cafeterias and other common areas with all the other children in the building but are assigned part of a corridor, or an entire floor perhaps, in which the classrooms for their mini-school are clustered.

JONATHAN KOZOL

This "solution," then, is not an answer to the physical decrepitude and overcrowding of these schools. An answer to *that* problem would cost billions of taxpayer dollars, which our states and cities cannot or do not intend to spend. Nor, of course, is it an answer to the racial isolation of the children in these schools. Indeed, in many cities, Seattle for example, the "mini-school" idea has been exploited by affluent white parents to create small, upscale, mainly white academies in neighborhoods in which their children otherwise might have to go to integrated high schools. And in New York, more flagrantly than elsewhere, mini-schools that have been broken off from larger schools in some of the city's racially mixed neighborhoods have rapidly been turned into exclusive sanctuaries for the children of the white and relatively affluent within a building in which almost all the other children are minorities.

Teachers in these schools report to me that if you walk into their building you can see an all-black small academy on one floor and a nearly all-white small academy one floor below. The curricula within these separate schools, the teachers say, differ dramatically. In some neighborhoods populated by large numbers of white people who are progressive in their educational beliefs (not, however, in their views on racial isolation), you will find what one teacher in the black part of her building teasingly refers to as "a woodsy Walden kind of school" primarily for white kids and a drill-and-kill academy, strictly geared to state exams, serving the children of color elsewhere in the building.

The "small schools" concept, if applied with care and forethought (and if school systems make sufficient space available), does have the virtue of reducing the disorder and the sense of hecticness I usually feel in visiting the massive high schools I've described. And because the teachers in a mini-school that serves perhaps only 200 students have a better chance to get to know each of those students fairly well, it helps reduce the sense of anonymity that students undergo in schools that hold as many as 4,000. There are plenty of other good things to be said of certain of these schools, the best of which (and this includes some of the smaller charter schools as well) tend to be progressive in their ethos and curricula and a few of which make serious efforts to achieve some class and racial mix within their student populations.

Still, as you have pointedly observed, no one is proposing that the richly academic high schools that are common in the towns where you and I grew up ought to be dismantled and replaced by "small academies." This is, in part, because these schools, while they may serve as many as 1,000 or even 2,000 students, do not try to pack in twice as many students as the school will hold, and they are well prepared to serve the number that they *do* enroll. Then, too, the parents of these students do not want to lose the amplitude of offerings that a large and broad-based faculty makes possible: ten or fifteen A.P. courses, for example, which are common in the good suburban high schools, often as many as five foreign languages, and wonderful art and theater workshops and orchestral music programs, all of which help to provide an entry-way to first-rate universities and colleges.

Sometimes, in order to compensate to some degree for the narrowness of expertise within their faculties, small academies whose parent leaders have good cultural connections manage to establish tie-ins with museums, theatrical and ballet groups, scientific institutions, and the like. Seattle's mostly white and upscale Center School, sited amidst the city's leading cultural attractions, is a classic instance of one of these new and well-connected small academies. Great inequities exist, however, between schools whose parent bodies and whose physical location make possible these exciting and attractive tie-ins and affiliations and, on the other hand, those small academies that serve exclusively black and Hispanic children in poor neighborhoods that are bereft of such prestigious institutions.

In an effort to disguise these inequalities, advocates for small schools in our urban systems often engage in an unseemly flattery of ghettoized communities by pointing to the "partnerships" that segregated small schools in such neighborhoods might now and then establish with black or Hispanic theater groups or, for example, African-American museums that might be in walking distance of these schools, if not to those corporate affiliations, which, as I've mentioned, seem increasingly to be the recipe of choice for schools that serve minorities.

But to romanticize poorly funded theater groups and other shoestring institutions in impoverished neighborhoods like the South Bronx, which does not even have a single Borders bookstore or a Barnes and Noble or, for that matter, a full-service bookstore of any kind at all to serve more than 600,000 people, almost all of color, does no favor to the children who are being rounded up to attend the small academies now being stamped out like so many formulaic products of a factory assembly-line in poverty communities.

"Blaming the victim" is, of course, anathema to those who view themselves as liberals or moderates politically and socially. But "flattering the victim" is a favorite practice nowadays, especially in white-owned media that constantly attempt to spare their segregated cities from the odium that they deserve, and their most valued readers from the guilt they otherwise might feel, by pointing to the slightest signs of cultural or economic self-rejuvenation in the neighborhoods to which their racial outcasts are consigned.

"Oh, they have a wealth of cultural resources, remarkable choirs, indigenous ballets . . . ," and this is true if we agree to look at these communities of destitution with the narrowest possible focus on a handful of specific institutions. I have worked closely with a number of these groups, which are often treasures in themselves, and have done everything I could, when I was asked, to reinforce and publicize their programs. But they are too few and far too poorly funded to provide a multitude of small academies with the richness and the continuity of offerings that well-supported boutique schools in neighborhoods like New York's Greenwich Village are provided by their geographical locations *and* by the clout that parents of their students bring to bear.

In any event, even if these problems of inequity could be transcended by the sponsorships provided on occasion by nonprofit groups, all the small schools that exist today and all of the next generation of such schools that are being contemplated for the ten years now ahead will serve no more than 5 or 10 percent of all the middle school and high school students in our inner-city neighborhoods. At best, Francesca, as you noted when you first arrived in Boston, this represents a minuscule, exceptionalist, and totally inadequate response to the tragedy of separate and unequal schooling in America.

Nonetheless, school administrators who are facing the persistent gap in skills between the students in their neighborhoods of color and those in the schools that serve the middle class and privileged are understandably prepared to climb aboard whatever new bandwagon is rolled out across the nation as the most recent "concept," the most trendy "innovation," or the most unreflectively promoted panacea. This is especially the case if the promoted panacea will not force them to make any reference to the segregated and unequal status quo they must defend—reference to which, many have assured me, would be most unwelcome in the business sector that can pull the string that ties the noose around their neck at any time it wants.

I have had repeated private conversations with administrators of our urban schools, including some who have run several of the largest districts in the course of their careers, and have heard them speak with utter candor, and a hearty dose of the same biting satire you've often employed, about the hype and overstatement used so commonly in the promotion of that seemingly eternal series of "solutions" that have floated in and out of fashion in the decades they have served.

In spite of this degree of post hoc honesty, most of these administrators feel obliged, while still in office, not just to comply with, but to actively support, whatever "new solution" is the flavor of the decade or the flavor of the year. This is all the more the case at the present moment when the wealthiest foundation in the nation, created by Bill and Melinda Gates, is offering large sums of money to those districts that are willing to establish small academies, regardless of the built-in flaws that we have seen and the deepened racial isolation to which many of these schools are now contributing.

I think I told you of a meeting that I had a couple years ago with a likable person named Tom Vander Ark, who was then in charge of setting education policy for the Gates Foundation, after he had listened to a presentation I had made, right there in his hometown of Seattle. I had made a plea to people in the audience not to yield to siren songs that seem to offer amiable, noncontroversial ways to do end runs around the hard reality of racial isolation in the nation's schools, which I said I viewed as an abiding cancer on the body of American democracy.

He approached me warmly at the end and wanted to chat with me, to my surprise, not about the plea that I'd just made but, he said, about an interest he had taken in the worth of "reading poetry." He said he'd never read much poetry as a young man but had recently been turned on to the poet Rilke. I was delighted, for a moment there, to have a chance to talk about one of the poets I revere—who, I have not forgotten, is one of your favorite poets too. Only later, when I was alone in my hotel, did it occur to me to wonder whether any of the points I had presented in my talk that night had got inside his head. I had the uncomfortable feeling that he somehow wrote off everything I'd said. Perhaps I didn't say it well. Perhaps he had concluded I was "a nice guy" but, in pedagogic terms, a naïve and romantic fool.

Not long after that, it was announced that the Gates Foundation had decided to invest a major portion of its education funding in the "new solution." We would soon have many more small, sometimes intimate and, on occasion, academically impressive segregated and unequal schools. Integration leaders in Seattle meanwhile told me with regret that Gates had given start-up money to The Center School, the elitist niche academy I mentioned to you earlier.

The Gates Foundation, with its vast resources, might yet transcend the damaging mistake that it has made if its leaders have the great maturity, not to say humility, to reexamine their precipitous decision and resolve instead, from this point on, to provide their grant support only to those small academies that formally commit themselves to an aggressive effort to reduce the racial isolation of the students they enroll. And, going beyond the small schools craze that it has helped to fan, the Gates Foundation might (and should) employ a hefty portion of its funds to give incentives to suburban districts, often no more than a ten- or twenty-minute drive from the most profoundly segregated urban areas, to underwrite an interdistrict integration movement modeled, for example, on the one in which I taught outside of Boston and which, for many years, has had effective counterparts in Louisville, St. Louis, and some other metropolitan communities.

All of these programs are now gravely threatened, as you know, by a tightening of purse strings at the local levels by state governments. They're also threatened by a ruling, which is going to be handed down by the Supreme Court very soon, which will likely cut off public money for all integration programs, even those that are entirely voluntary, are stalwartly defended by participating suburbs, have waiting lists of thousands of black and Hispanic children hoping, against all odds, to get into better-funded and successful schools. (The director of the program here in Boston told me recently that 16,000 kids are on the waiting list. That's nearly a third of all the children of color in this city.)

This, then, is a situation where a large foundation could, by its incentives, do something authentically courageous that wouldn't merely tinker with the edges of injustice but might wield a very big sledgehammer in the struggle to transform the racial status quo. I can hear you telling me, "Don't hold your breath!" I won't. But I've been surprised at least a few times in my life by the willingness of people with tremendous power to rethink their own beliefs and change directions in a course they've already selected.

Maybe if a large group of determined teachers and school principals like many I know in Seattle, maybe religious leaders too, and thousands of other decent citizens who believe that "separate but equal" education did not work during the more than one hundred years since it began and will work no better in the hundred years ahead, were to descend upon the Gates Foundation with this message, it might have a good effect. Or maybe not. . . .

Perhaps it will take a great deal more than isolated protests on the part of gutsy teachers and their allies in one city or one region of the nation if we are to make our voices heard. Marian Wright Edelman, one of the friends whose judgment I have always trusted most, believes we need another civil rights upheaval in this nation to reverse the backward slide we've seen during these recent years. Her personal history of struggle in the South, now more than 40 years ago, fuels her conviction that it takes a massive and inspired movement of impassioned activists to stir a nation from its slumber when elected leaders lack the moral fortitude to act upon an ethical abomination on their own.

On days when I'm discouraged it's not easy to imagine such a national upheaval at this moment in our history, when many teachers and most other advocates for children seem to feel so much on the defensive and when forces of conservative triumphalism seem to be riding high and trampling freely over almost everything that you and I believe. What I dearly hope is that young people like yourself will prove me wrong. And if you do—and if it's actually going to happen—I hope it happens soon. I'd like to be around to be a part of it.

CHAPTER FOURTEEN

Teachers as Witnesses

Dear Francesca,

Nearly eight months have passed since we began these conversations. I was excited when you told me you are going to be promoted with your children to the second grade next fall. You said it's known as "looping" and that you might go with them to third grade after that or else come back and start out with a new class of first graders.

Anyway, this means you'll have Shaniqua, Dobie, and Arturo, and your other children with you for another year. I'm glad your principal agreed to this. When something good is happening between a teacher and her class, why bring it to an end?

I've been thinking that I should no longer speak of you as a "beginning" teacher. You seem so comfortable and self-possessed by now that, even though you say you know you still have much to learn, you already have that sense of earned authority that I described in speaking about seasoned teachers such as Frances Dukes. And because your principal shares many of your views on education policies, I think she's helped empower you (at least she hasn't tried to undermine the feeling of empowerment that you somehow acquired on your own) to say what you believe and vent your furies on these matters when you need to.

But many other teachers who confide in me, in letters and in phone calls and in meetings at their schools, are not in situations as convivial or as empowering as yours. Typically, they've been assigned to low-performing schools whose principals have felt they need to buckle under to the warnings and the mandates of the new accountability regimes imposed by Washington or by their local boards of education. The risk these teachers face of being fired if they deviate from these demands induces them too often to suppress their discontent and to accommodate themselves to teaching methods which they know would never have been tolerated in the good suburban schools that they attended.

Some of the same teachers, who now find themselves in schools where every child in the building is black or Hispanic, also speak to me about the disappointment that they feel at seeing this regression to an older order of accepted and of uncontested segregated education, with the inequalities that are endemic to such schooling and which are self-evident to them right from the start. But they also speak of being cautioned by their older friends or other teachers in their schools about the danger—or the sheer futility—of giving voice to discontents like these too openly. Sometimes it's their parents who convey this sense of danger to them in the strongest terms. Their parents often didn't want them to go into teaching to begin with. Now that they have made this choice, their parents do not want to see them doing things, or saying things, that might imperil their careers.

I always want to tell these young idealists that the world is not as dangerous as many in the older generation want them to believe. This is a big country, with 93,000 public schools in 14,000 districts, many of which are run by good administrators who have very much the same concerns as they. Virtually every teacher I have known who's lost a job over a point of moral principle has ended up with a better job within less than a year. The teachers for whom I feel the greatest sadness are the ones who choke on their beliefs, who never act on their ideals, who never know the taste of struggle in a decent cause and never know the thrill of even partial victories.

So I come back again and again to the need for teachers to speak out as witnesses to what they see each day before their eyes, whether they do this only in the most restrained and quiet ways at schoolwide gatherings or meetings in the districts where they work or in bolder voices at the larger education conferences and in the education journals and the mainstream media. "Witnessing" is a familiar term among the clergy of progressive and compassionate denominations. As I've said to you before, I think it ought to be the privilege, and obligation, of our teachers too.

Perhaps this is the right time to go back and say a few last words about my own timidity when I first walked into the school in which I started my career so many years ago in Roxbury. The truth is, I was very wary about causing problems for myself and was therefore much too cautious at the start about condemning practices that struck me as distasteful or, in the case of children who were taken to the basement to be whipped, as outrightly sadistic. In retrospect, I feel I was complicit in these practices because I permitted students in the first class that I taught to be subjected to these punishments.

It wasn't until the spring, when I was transferred to the class that had already had 12 teachers, and had, as a consequence, lost nearly a year of education, that I started saying certain things to children in my room and taking actions outside of the school that were very tentatively adversarial in terms of my relationship to the administration. I've told you, for example, of the visits I began to make to children's homes, which disturbed my principal, but her reaction was at most admonitory and it was conveyed in words that seemed to be intended for my own protection.

It was only in the last weeks of the year that I became sufficiently emboldened to do something that I now can see turned out to be directly confrontational;

and, even then, I stumbled into it almost by accident and with little forethought of the anger and the controversy it was likely to create.

One day at a store in Harvard Square, I saw a new hardcover book of poetry by Langston Hughes, whom, as I told you, I had never heard about until that year. I picked it up and read it through that night and marked some poems that I particularly liked, and brought it with me the next morning into school. I thought my students, some of them at least, would take an interest in these poems; but the reaction of the children to the very presence of that book within my hand when they walked into class exceeded anything that I could ever have anticipated. Even before I opened the book, the children noticed the photo of the author on the cover. "Look!" one of the children in the front row whispered to a child next to her. "That man is colored!"

I read a few poems from the book, including one about a black man who refused to pay his rent until his landlord would repair his leaking roof and broken stairs. It ended with the man's eviction and arrest, a situation with which children in that neighborhood could easily identify. I also read the well-known poem "A Dream Deferred," which I think you told me that you've read to your class too.

There was one student in that class, a beautiful girl with a chiseled-looking jaw, who was taller than the other children in the room and who, no matter what I'd tried to do to win her interest in the weeks up to that time, would never open up to me. She insisted upon sitting in the back row of the room and had a look of bitter vigilance and of unyielding hardness in her eyes. It occurred to me that she alone, of all the children in the class, had somehow come to understand the full extent of what the school had done to her that year and could not forgive me, as a white man and a grown-up, for the damage she had undergone.

But, in the silence after I had read "A Dream Deferred," something quite remarkable occurred. This stoic-looking child who had been so hostile to me for so long quietly got up from her chair, walked around the five rows that divided us, came right up to my side, and with the greatest dignity, and with the poise and confidence of somebody much older, she gently touched me on my arm and asked if I would let her bring the book home so that she could show it to her mother.

The following day, before the class began, she told me she had memorized the poem the night before. After asking my permission, she then stood there by my desk and recited it to the entire class. The rock of ice that had encased her all year long broke suddenly. That look of vigilance, at least for now, was gone.

Francesca, I think I should emphasize again that I had not thought through what I was doing when I brought that book to class. I do know it mattered to me that the author of the book was African-American, because there was not a single book or even a short passage in a text by a black author in that room. I also wanted the students in my class to see a new and handsome-looking book, a book that had the crisp, exciting ink smell of a newly published work, because all the books and textbooks in the room were old and tattered—"raggedy," as the children liked to say—and bore publication dates from ten or twenty years before.

I wanted to get across to them the sense that reading need not be a dull and deadening encounter with gray ink in parallel columns in a tired-looking text, with "unit questions" every seven pages, but can be a wonderful and fresh encounter with something that's powerful and stirring and has also been designed to be attractive to a reader. So there was nothing either very brave or very bold in what I'd done; yet I also had the premonition that I might be forced to pay a price for doing this.

My premonition proved to be correct. Scarcely a week later, I was called into the office of the principal and told by her that what I'd done was reprehensible and that, for this reason, I was being fired from my job. Her immediate superior within the Boston schools said that, because of this infraction, I would never be allowed to teach in any Boston school again. The formal charge against me was "curriculum deviation," because the poems of Langston Hughes I'd read, as it turned out, were not included in the course of study stipulated for fourth grade.

Earlier in the spring, as you'll recall, I'd read my students poems by Robert Frost and William Butler

Yeats, which were not included in the course of study either. The principal had expressed no disapproval of these poems and, indeed, had mentioned passingly that she was glad that I was introducing Robert Frost to my fourth graders because this might help to counteract what she regarded as the lack of culture in their homes. The poetry of Langston Hughes, however, as one of the deputy superintendents soon made clear, fell into a different category altogether.

"We cannot give directives to the teachers to use literature written in native dialects," this official said. "We are trying to break the speech patterns of these children, trying to get them to speak properly." The poem about the tenant and his landlord, in particular, she said, "does not present correct grammatical expression and would just entrench the speech patterns we want to break."

A member of the Boston School Committee later issued a report in which he said that teachers like myself were commonly dismissed because they were found "unsuitable in training, personality, or character." Any individual "who lacks the personal discipline to abide by rules and regulations, as we all must in our civilized society, is obviously unsuited for the highly responsible profession of teaching," he concluded. Ten years later, the man who issued this report, a politically ambitious man named Thomas Eisenstadt, was forced to call an end to his political career after having been exposed for theft of public funds.

I had been forbidden by my principal to say goodbye to my students or to tell them I had been dismissed. At the end of class, however, a child who liked to stay behind with me after the other kids were gone helped me to pile up my books and pictures and the map of Paris and the other posters with which I had tried to decorate the room. Outside the school, on the sidewalk, as she helped me pack these things into my car, I said goodbye to her and told her, as she must have understood by then, that I would not be back. When she asked me why, I told her only that I'd had a disagreement with the principal. I asked her to say goodbye for me to all the other children. She took what I said with great solemnity and promised that she would relay my message.

As soon as I got home, I telephoned Jim Breeden, an Episcopal priest who was the de facto leader of the civil rights groups in the black community and who had befriended me earlier that year. A generally mild and understated man, he became incensed when I explained the reason why I had been fired.

Word, from that point on, spread quickly through the neighborhood, and some of the parents of my students, with the help of local organizers, went from door to door to tell the other parents what had taken place that afternoon. If they got no answer at the front door they'd knock at the kitchen door. If no one was home they'd leave a message with a neighbor. The message they left was simply this: A teacher had been fired from their school for reading their children "a good poem written by a Negro." The reaction of the parents startled me by its intensity.

A meeting was called at a local church to which the parents asked if I would come in order to relate the series of events that led to my dismissal. They also asked me to describe the textbooks I had found in class when I arrived, the overall atmosphere within the school, and other elements of the scenario of deprivation to which children in the building were exposed.

I remember feeling frightened suddenly. I arrived late at the meeting and it took the coaxing of one of the mothers I had come to know that year to give me the nerve to overcome my shyness about entering the church. When I did go in, I found the largest gathering of parents I had ever seen assembled in the neighborhood or at the school in that entire year. Instead of the 15 or 20 or, occasionally, 30 parents who might show up at a meeting of the PTA, there were about 200 parents in the room, including more than half the parents of the children in my class. Several of the kids to whom I hadn't been allowed to say goodbye were sitting in the front row.

The head of the Boston NAACP, which had helped the parents organize the meeting, saw that I was nervous and he placed his arm protectively over my shoulder as he led me to the stage. When he said it was my turn to speak, I did the best I could to overcome my fear. As a white man from outside the neighborhood, I wasn't sure I had the right to fill the role in which I found myself. And seeing my students sitting there before me, some of whom were crying, was so stirring to me that I found it hard to summon up more than a few brief words. Whatever I said, the parents seemed to understand the reasons for my shyness. Some of the close friendships that I made that night have lasted for a lifetime.

On the Monday after my firing, about two dozen parents of my students kept their children home in protest and went up to school to take their children's places in their chairs. A week later, a much larger protest took place outside of the office of the Boston School Committee. Several thousand people, not only blacks but many whites as well this time, marched in the glare of TV lights to send a message to the city's leaders that they would no longer tolerate in silence the destruction of the spirits of so many children for no reason but the accident of birth.

I tell this story sometimes to young teachers who grew up, as you and I did, in a white and affluent community and now work in inner-city schools. I urge them not to underestimate the decency and loyalty that they will find, if they ever end up in a situation like the one I faced, among the parents of an African-American community. Despite the sometimes seemingly divisive Afro-centric rhetoric one hears, inner-city parents in my own experience are seldom blinded by skin color when it comes to what they think to be their children's own well-being.

Distinctions of ethnicity become the last things

on their minds if they believe that we are doing everything we can to help their kids survive an education system which, as they know all too well from their own years of childhood, has very rarely given people of their race an even chance. Even if they see that we are inexperienced or, as in my case, almost wholly unprepared, most of the parents I have come to know throughout these years are quick to recognize when teachers, of whatever racial background we may be, are committed to their children.

The very warm extended family you've created with the parents of your children during the past year, and the loyalty and fondness they have shown for you, are things that education students seldom hear about in courses on ethnicity and race, in which the factors that divide us get a great deal more attention than the commonality of interests that unite us. But the powerful sense of solidarity you get from parents at your classroom meetings, including parents who are strongest in the affirmation of their own ethnicity, ought to send a message to young teachers who have been intimidated by the kind of sociology that is supposed to heighten "sensitivity to differences" but, because it's sometimes taught so heavy-handedly, ends up by manufacturing gratuitous anxieties.

I wish these students could be given more exposure to young teachers who have taught in situations like your own and have no time to waste in using overblown vocabularies about "hegemonic differences" to deepen ethnic lines but who, instead, by hard work, love, and their inherent sensibilities, have learned the ways to *cross* those lines and, when they did, found graciousness and generosity awaiting them.

Francesca, I think I would be remiss if I didn't add here, as a postscript to this letter, that I certainly am not presenting my experience in Boston as a model for "strategic intervention" on the part of other teachers. The point is not to lose your job! It is to find a way to navigate the contradictions it presents without entirely forfeiting one's personality or undermining the ideals that make our work with children "a vocation" in the truest sense rather than a slotted role within a spiritless career.

Most schools, in any case, are not as medieval or as brutal as the one in which I worked. Most principals are not contemptuous of parents in their neighborhoods. Most administrative leaders are not racists, and very few whom I have come to know are as despotic as the ones who ran the Boston schools in 1965. There is usually a little room for "wiggly" and "wobbly" to find their way into the timelines that we teach. There is usually room for caterpillars and for other furry creatures and stuffed animals with comforting expressions to provide our children with reminders that they *are* still children and are treasured for that reason. There are usually at least some openings, as well, for deviation from that straight line of prescribed intentionality, and many teachers learn to

JONATHAN KOZOL

camouflage their deviations with sufficient ingenuity as to protect themselves from getting more attention than they'd like.

If all else fails, however, and a teacher has been left with no alternative but to denounce intolerable practices in explicit and straightforward terms and is dismissed or threatened with dismissal as a consequence, I don't think that he or she ought to accept this passively. I think they ought to seize this moment as an opportunity to pinpoint and illuminate a body of destructive policies that would offend and shock most sensible Americans. In other words, I think that teachers who are thrust into this situation ought to be prepared to speak and act politically. I say this even though I know it's difficult for almost anyone who doesn't have the moral temperament you do, as well as the tremendous faith you have in your political beliefs, even to contemplate this possibility.

Many teachers who have grown up steeped in the traditions and the history of civil rights, the words of the great leaders and their instances of courage, and the many sacrifices they have made, and who find themselves today in situations that require courage of their own, tell me of the inner struggle they have faced to reconcile their calling as a teacher, and the relatively quiet and noncontroversial nature of the role this is expected to imply, with that "other calling" as a witness to injustice in our public schools, to which they are almost always the *best* witnesses.

Most of these teachers are familiar with the well-known words of Dr. King: "I've been to the mountaintop . . . and I've seen the promised land." Many post these words, which Dr. King spoke on the eve of his assassination, on their classroom walls, often in the high schools in a class on U.S. history and government, or in the elementary schools in January when the birth of Dr. King is celebrated.

At the same time, however, almost every public voice we've heard for more than 20 years has counseled us to shut the mountain out of view and to direct our eyes instead to the less problematic flatlands where careers are made and résumés are typed and individual security may be protected and advanced. That may be one reason why it's so much harder now for youthful teachers to invite the risks that people of their age were willing to incur when cries of "Freedom Now" were in the air and ethically transcendent leaders like John Lewis and Bob Moses, not to speak of Dr. King himself, inspired them to place their bodies on the line to act on their beliefs.

This is why I find myself encouraging the strongest-hearted teachers that I know to start the work of building a coherent oppositional mentality that will reinforce the willingness of other teachers to speak out not just as educators but also as public citizens. I have seen groups of teachers doing this already in a number of our major cities, where they're reaching out to previously less vocal teachers and, wherever possible, to principals and empathetic educators in the universities, as well as to students in the education schools. Their objective is to build a network of politi-cally sophisticated educators to resist the punitive and racially discriminating practices that are being forced upon them by the state and federal governments.

There are those in Washington and elsewhere who believe that teachers are already "too political." I could not more deeply disagree. I think the problem is exactly the reverse. Teachers, in their larger num-bers, aren't nearly political *enough*. (I'm not speaking about teacher unions, which are, and ought to be, po-litical, but about the teacher in and of herself, or him-self, as an individual.)

I don't mean by this that teachers in our public schools do not, in general, have strong political con-victions. What I mean is that too many have no knowledge of the things that they can actually *do*—the strategies that activists in other eras of our history have counted on—to alter the conditions they per-ceive. Even those who aren't intimidated in the least by the purported dangers they may face if they take actions consonant with their beliefs have, too often, no idea at all of how to go about this.

There are also teachers, fortunately a smaller number, who have attended education schools that are reminiscent, in the culture of timidity and self-concealment they unwittingly promote, of some of the teacher-training colleges of the 1950s and preceding decades, in which future teachers are indoctrinated to behave as if they have no passionate opinions about almost anything at all that might conceivably be viewed as controversial. Some of these teachers have been victimized, as well, by being counseled to behave as if they have no vital or exciting private lives or any frolicsome and possibly subversive eccentricities. In a sense, they've neutered both their politics and personalities to a degree. Some do rebel against the antiseptic state of mind to which they've been conditioned. Others cannot seem to break out of the glaze by which their personalities have been surrounded.

The future teachers I try to recruit are those who have refused to let themselves be neutered in this way, either in their private lives or in the lives that they intend to lead at school. When they begin to teach, they come into their classrooms with a sense of affirmation of the goodness and the fullness of existence, with a sense of satisfaction in discovering the unexpected in their students, and with a longing to surprise the world, their kids, even themselves, with their capacity to leave each place they've been (a school, a classroom, a community of learning) a better and more joyful place than it was when they entered it.

These are the kinds of glowing souls who tend to win the love of children almost without effort. But those who are recipients of children's love take on responsibilities they sometimes can't anticipate. One of those responsibilities, I think, is the willingness to do away with any semblance of what they may have been taught to think of as "professional decorum," when such a moment may be called for, and instead to act, no matter what their shyness or their modest self-effacement, as outspoken warriors for justice.

Francesca, I have told you of the hesitation and timidity I felt for most of my first year in Boston. You've already shown a lot more healthy nerve than I did in that situation. But the generation of young teachers who are entering these schools today may need more courage than the two of us combined. A battle is beginning for the soul of education, and they must be its ultimate defenders.

CHAPTER FIFTEEN

Seeds of Hope,
Sources of Resilience

Dear Francesca,

Last October, after I had visited your class for the first time, you mentioned that you were surprised—I think you might have said "relieved"—that I didn't seem to be the very serious and solemn kind of person you expected me to be.

Other teachers who have read my books before we met have told me the same thing. Some of them say that if they read one of my recent books before they go to bed, the stories that I tell about the children sadden them or else infuriate them so much that it makes it hard for them to sleep.

So when they meet me they're surprised to find I'm not the grim and gloomy person they expect. They want to know how I can spend so many hours tramping through so many truly awful schools, going down into the basement lunchrooms with the children, sitting through interminable drilling sessions in their classes, and then heading down to Washington as I have done again and again since 1968 to testify in front of subcommittees of the House or Senate to present my pleas for changes in official policies that have been harmful to these children—and almost always coming home with an exquisite sense of absolute defeat—without emerging in a state of permanent depression.

There is at least one answer to this question that I know will not surprise you. It has to do with the exhilaration that I get out of my day-to-day immersion in the lives of certain glowingly resilient children who, no matter what the painful things they may experience at school or in their homes, are able somehow to retain their faith in the essential goodness of the grown-up world and to keep their little lights of hope alive. "I ain't dead though, am I?" said the piper; and these are children who refuse to let their spirits be destroyed by even the most formidable situations of injustice that surround them. When it comes to courage, my best teachers have been children.

Then, too, the ordinary details of their lives, the twisty reddish licorice sticks they buy at the bodegas or the corner stores, the blue and white and yellow beads and butterflies their mothers weave so lovingly into the braidings of their hair, the utterly unexpected questions that they ask me, and the things that they find funny (which I usually find funny too) are like tiny pieces of soul nourishment for anyone whose spirit may be heavy with concerns of which the children do not know.

A six-year-old in the South Bronx named Mario, another of the little boys, like Dobie, whose father was in prison and who in a tender way adopted me to be his "uncle" or his grown-up friend for several years, once whispered something to a child in his class named Tabitha which she said that she considered "very, very bad." Since I'd always thought of Mario as a rather innocent and gentle child, I could not resist the urge to ask her what he'd said. "Fishy, fishy!" she replied, which sent her off into a gale of laughter she could not control. When she had recovered temporarily, she covered up her face with her two arms and shook her head repeatedly at the sheer naughtiness these words seemed to imply.

"That doesn't seem so bad," I said.

"It's bad! It is!" she said and fell into another episode of helpless laughter once again.

The next day, at P.S. 30, I was talking with her principal about a set of guidelines on curriculum revisions that the school had just received; but I wasn't really concentrating on the issues that the principal had raised. "Fishy, fishy" kept on going through my mind. I was trying to guess what secret wickedness those words might hold for Tabitha and Mario. The issues that will shape the fate of children in these schools are large, but the details of their lives are intimate and small. It is in the tender nature of those intimate particulars that, for me, a salvatory sense of fascination and a feeling of persistent optimism manage to survive.

My gloriously independent-minded friend Pineapple was, for me, a package of emotional salvation in and of herself. A bossy little person, she attracted my attention first when she was five years old in kindergarten class. By the third or fourth time that we met— she was in third grade by now—she was blunt enough to tell me that she didn't like the woolen jersey I was wearing. She plucked at it with her finger, making clear her discontent. She also asked me if the old and shabby-looking black suit that I usually wore was the only one I had. I told her I had two suits but that they were both nearly the same.

She must have thought about this for a while because later, at the St. Ann's afterschool, she sat me down and told me, in so many words, "You need to go and buy another suit. I like to see you when you look respectable." When I showed up a few months later in a new suit that was the same color as the one I'd worn before, she registered her disappointment instantly. "Jonathan," she told me in the kindest and most earnest voice, "I know that you feel sad sometimes, but you don't always need to dress in black."

Pineapple had a high respect for matters of propriety. One steamy day in August when I joined a group of children from the South Bronx on a field trip to Manhattan for an afternoon of games in Central

Park, Pineapple came over, looking very hot and thirsty, and flopped down beside me on the grass. Not far from us, in a shaded area beside a walking path, there was a vendor selling sodas, juice, and snacks. I saw Pineapple looking off from time to time in his direction.

At that point, I made a bad mistake in judgment. Instead of getting up and going with Pineapple to the stand to buy some juice for both of us, I took my wallet from my pocket, handed her the smallest bill I had, which was ten dollars, and suggested without thinking that she go and buy herself some juice or soda to relieve her thirst.

Pineapple studied the ten-dollar bill, then said, "Excuse me," and got up to find her older sister, who was standing with a group of teenage girls. The two girls wandered off a ways and seemed to have a kind of "conference," and I saw Pineapple nodding while her sister talked. Then she bashfully returned to me and, holding out the money, said her mother wouldn't want her to accept it but that "it would be okay" if I would like to get some juice—"because *you* must be thirsty"—and, if I did, it would be nice if I would like to buy some for her too.

I got up and went with her to buy the juice for both of us and once she had that icy bottle in her hand, she gulped it down before I'd even opened mine.

Even then, I felt embarrassed by the way I'd handled things. Giving her ten dollars, which was quite a lot of money to a child in her neighborhood, had been a clumsy act. It had unsettled her by its excessiveness, as well as by the fact that it was a direct transaction, and it had offended against good advice she had been given by her mother. Allowing me to buy cold drinks for both of us, a normal thing to do on a hot summer afternoon, appeared more natural to her and posed no questions about manners or proprieties.

I remember feeling chastised by her hesitation and I think she knew this. I think the reason she had gone off to discuss this with her sister was that she did not want to embarrass me, or hurt my feelings, but she also wanted very much to figure out a way to get something to drink! Their brief negotiation session seemed to have resolved it.

Moments like this, when Pineapple's good manners and respect for what her mother had instructed her came across so clearly, intensified my fondness for this child. And the clever way she'd handled this (both of us, I think, were conscious of the slightly comic undercurrent that was running through our efforts to get something cold to drink for both of us) amused me just enough so that my feelings of embarrassment soon disappeared.

Pineapple was a leader among children in the neighborhood and now and then she exercised her leadership position somewhat autocratically. On the train returning to the Bronx from Central Park that afternoon, I noticed that she struck a rather haughty and authoritative pose. One hand on her hip, one holding to the pole, her sneakers pointed out in opposite directions, she oversaw the antics of the restless boys, who kept on switching seats and getting in the way of other passengers, with barely tolerant disdain. Now and then, she'd make a snappish comment, which she often did too harshly with the younger children; but when she did this she would almost always recognize if she had gone too far and, after some blustery resistance, would apologize.

To this day, when I am low in spirit, I try to arrange my visits to New York so that I can have a chance to get together with Pineapple, sometimes with her sisters and her parents, sometimes just the two of us alone. She's a competent teenager now and speaks to me less as her teacher or grown-up adviser and more as a friend. The political frustrations that I often feel evaporate when I am with her for a while.

Some of the young white students whom I meet in education schools, while sensitive in other ways, may be inclined to think of working with low-income children in the inner cities as a purely altruistic act, an ethical and social benediction they can bring to those less fortunate than they. It's never seemed like that to me, and I know it's never been like that for you. I've never felt that I was heading to the South Bronx with a bag of blessings, intellectual or otherwise, imported straight from Harvard Square, to scatter on the foreheads of the children of the poor. I've always felt that I was going there in *search* of blessings, and in the personalities of children like Pineapple and the playfulness and sweetness of the younger ones like Tabitha and Mario, I feel I've found those blessings every time.

In spite of the familiar stereotype of mean and disrespectful inner-city kids perpetuated often by the media, especially TV, most of the inner-city children I have known show great respect for people like myself who come to visit from outside their neighborhoods, and they are especially solicitous of older people who are physically more vulnerable than they. When he was only seven years old, Mario used to ask me to sit down and rest when I would show up at the after-school at St. Ann's Church feeling frayed and weary if I'd come directly from the airport or the train. He'd ask me if I'd like a plate of cookies or a glass of juice and, even before I answered, he'd run off into the kitchen to find something he thought would be good for me.

One night, when he was nine, he saw me walking in the neighborhood when I was heading for the train. He immediately became concerned by this and asked if he could walk me to the station at Brook Avenue, which was at that time one of the busiest marketplaces for the crack trade in the area. I told him that I'd made that walk repeatedly and that I had never had a problem at Brook Avenue. He accepted this reluctantly. "Cuidate, Jonathan!" he cautioned me—"Be careful!"—as we said goodbye.

The enduring friendships of these children are my sustenance, Francesca. Their capability to rise above the grim environment in which they live—the physical illnesses that are so common in their neighborhood, the pediatric asthma and the epidemic levels of maternal HIV, not even to speak of the narcotics trade that flourishes around them—the affirmation by these children of the possibilities for life and hope in the immediate proximity of so much death and pain always makes me feel ashamed of my own periodic moments of self-pity and it clears my spirits of depression and morbidity.

Some years ago, I visited a third grade class at P.S. 65 taught by a teacher, Angie Gallombardo, who had come to be a friend of mine. I think I've mentioned her to you before, because her natural rapport with children was a lot like yours, and she was the only teacher in the building at the time who talked to me openly about the problems in the school.

Only a few months earlier, a child named Bernardo, who had been a student at the school, had died by falling down the elevator shaft of his apartment building, which was almost next door to the school, after parents on his floor had told the building manager on more than one occasion that the elevator door was not attached correctly and flew open if somebody pressed against it by mistake. Bernardo, who was only eight, forgot the warnings he'd been given by his family, accidentally leaned against the door one day, and plunged four stories through the open shaft until he struck the steel roof of the elevator. His body wasn't found until his blood began to drip on passengers.

I had visited Bernardo's family on the night before my visit to Ms. Gallombardo's class. So when I came into her room that day I was in a somber state of mind and wondered whether I could get my spirits "up" enough to be a good participant in the activities that she had planned. It turned out that the children made this easy. They had already undergone a period of mourning for their friend and, although his name did come up once while I was there, they had largely set the sorrow of this tragedy behind them by this time, and the atmosphere within the classroom would not have allowed a stranger to suspect the sadness they had recently been through.

The children had been told I was a writer and, like many children who quite often make this flattering mistake, they thought this was incredibly exciting and had carefully prepared a bunch of questions that they fired at me energetically, like just so many eight-year-old reporters. The questions they asked were really interesting to me and were, in fact, a whole lot more original than the questions grown-up interviewers generally pose.

"Is it lonesome to write?"

"How do you write so many words?"

"How do you feel if people criticize your books?"

"Does it make you sad when people know your books but can't pronounce your name?"

"Do you feel sad because you're old?"

One of the children also asked, "Do you write little books or chapter books?"

I had forgotten that distinction between books that are, essentially, extended stories and books long enough to be divided into chapters. Although I'd never thought of it this way before, I told the children, "I write chapter books," which led one of them to ask me why I didn't also write what she called "easy books" for younger children.

I answered that I'd never done that yet because I think it takes a special gift that I don't have but that I would like to try to write a book like that someday.

"Do it!" the child said, dispensing briskly with my effort to be self-effacing.

The teacher said the children in the class were also writers—several were writing "real books," she reported—and that this was why they'd put a lot of thought into preparing questions for me.

I answered the other questions they had asked the best I could. No, I said, I didn't mind if people can't pronounce my name, because most people find it hard to know which syllable to emphasize. I said it did upset me to be criticized, with which the children seemed to empathize. They said it hurt their feelings too, even though they knew that this would help them do a better job on their revisions, which I said was true in my case too. And "yes," I told them, "writing can be very lonesome, that's the hardest part of it for me," but writing "many words" is not so hard once you begin "and sometimes it's much harder to write something short that's really good than something long."

I dodged the question about being "old" and

asked if they would tell me more about the books that they were writing, at which point they took their folders out and let me read their books and see the pictures they had drawn to go with them. One of the children asked me how a writer gets a publisher and, when I said I had an agent who helps me decide each time if what I've done is good enough to show a publisher, this persistent little boy asked me for my agent's name and her address.

Bernardo's death, the result of a long history of gross neglect on the part of a man who owned another 37 run-down buildings in the neighborhood (and, I was embarrassed to find out, lives in Massachusetts in the town where I grew up, where he is regarded as a generous philanthropist), remained a burning issue for me, as for parent leaders in the neighborhood, for many months to come. But in the hours when I was with those children I am glad to say that I was thinking not of death and tragedy but of vitality and curiosity, and of the children's creativity. And when that child asked me for my agent's name and her address, his juvenile bravado struck me as so wonderfully audacious that I sat right down and wrote it out for him, although his teacher later told me he decided that "it might be premature" (the teacher's words) to follow up on this for now.

Teachers in other inner-city schools often tell their kids that I'm a writer, since they want to spur their students to believe they can be writers too. The children always ask me questions about how I write, and why I write, and where I live, and who my mother is, and if I have a dog, and what she's like, and whether I have children (it disappoints them when I say I don't), but they do not ask me why I like to be with them. One of the nicest qualities most of these children have is generous discretion. I'm grateful that they leave some pleasant things unquestioned.

Francesca, I don't need to tell you, of all people, that it's hard for anyone to stay depressed for long if he or she has had the opportunity to spend so many hours in the company of children. When Pineapple sat me down that time and counseled me about the dark and formal clothes I wore (I still recall the firm, authoritative way she folded her arms against her chest as the two of us sat face-to-face), I was taken aback at first. But then the irony of the situation, a child living in the dreariest of neighborhoods counseling a grown-up man, essentially, "to lighten up," seemed like such a nice reversal of our roles that it left me smiling at myself. Her kindly message ("you don't always need to dress in black") also struck me as such good advice that I wrote her words down and went home and posted them above my desk next to the words of other buoyant spirits, like Thoreau.

But there's another reason why my sense of hope and energy and a determination to persist in what has been a life-long struggle seldom flag. This has to do not with the kids themselves but with many of their parents and, more to the point in neighborhoods like Roxbury and the South Bronx, their often very strong grandparents.

I don't want to overstate this point because, as you have noted more than a few times, the inclination of some white progressives to romanticize the families in black and Hispanic neighborhoods has a disconcerting quality, as if they feel obliged to counteract the unattractive stereotypes they've heard by describing almost every inner-city parent or grandparent as sublimely noble, eloquent, and wise. This is obviously not true, as you and I have both discovered in the case of members of some of our students' families who have been so damaged by the missteps they have taken or the obstacles they have encountered that their voices have been muted and their capability for making wise decisions has been seriously impaired.

Still, I have been fortunate throughout the years of my career to know a lot of parents and grandparents whose intrinsic strength and whose ability for affirmation, even when it's hard to know exactly what they *can* affirm, has been a source of consolation to me and a potent antidote to the discouragement and sometimes paralyzing sense of isolation that so many social activists and educators feel when they survey the panorama of regressive forces that surround us.

I've described a number of grandmothers in the South Bronx in two of the books I've written about children living in that neighborhood, both of which, Ordinary Resurrections and Amazing Grace, I know you've read. But what I've never said explicitly before is that I have turned to several of these women when I have been facing problems that had no connection with the various crises of their children and grandchildren but were related solely to anxieties and worries in my private life. One of the grandmothers who lives near Pineapple's building, a woman named Bernice King, who helps to run the kitchen at St. Ann's and to prepare the dinner given to the children at the afterschool, has taken me into her home on evenings when she recognized I wasn't feeling well and had lost the sense of generally good spirits that have typically propelled me through the long days I have spent with children in the neighborhood.

During a time in which my mother, who was in her nineties, had grown very frail and my father, who had been a prominent neurologist, a specialist in brain deterioration, had been diagnosed with Alzheimer's and no longer recognized me when I went to visit at his nursing home, Bernice became a mother to me in the purest sense of making her home a sanctuary for me and a place where I could talk about my mom and dad, and the fear of losing other people who were close to me, in ways I never talked to anybody else.

Bernice is also an outrageous gossip. So our evenings at her kitchen table would be richly flavored with long sagas of the peccadilloes and internal rivalries and jealousies and wild misadventures of some of the people in the neighborhood she knew and liked but never wholly trusted for good reasons of her own.

Sometimes we'd talk as late as 2:00 a.m. and then she would insist on walking with me to Brook Avenue and waiting with me for the train. At that late hour, when drug-dealers in their hooded sweatshirts tended to hang out around the subway steps, I did not refuse Bernice's offer.

Every time I spend an evening with Bernice, I come away feeling restored. She's often said my visits give her strength as well, because she questions me about the medical problems that she has to deal with, as well as the education problems her grandchildren face. I'm glad when I can draw upon resources that she does not have to set up introductions for her to another person who can help her find her way, for instance, through the labyrinth of the healthcare system in the Bronx. The mutuality of help and sustenance between us has continued to this day.

Whenever I tell myself that it just seems too hard or hopeless to continue trying to keep up the battle to defend the values you and I hold dear and to go out in public, when I have to, and debate those very agile and sometimes sadistically effective people from the right-wing think tanks, which is no fun at all, I think of the indomitable courage of so many older women like Bernice, who face not merely trivial and one-time injuries or disappointments or political reversals, but extremes of physical discomfort from untreated illnesses as well as psychological ordeals that most of us can only empathetically imagine.

This, Francesca, is the ultimate answer to the question that you posed. I don't believe that any of us has the right to pull back from the battlefield because we're feeling "weary." And the truth is that I *don't* feel weary, not for long at least, after I've been with a good friend like Bernice or had some time to be with children like Pineapple, Tabitha, and Mario, or like Bernardo's schoolmates. (How could anybody remain weary or depressed for long after an encounter with a child like that boy who managed to extract my agent's name and her address from me, which very few writers, even those of my own age, have ever done successfully?)

I gain the same sense of renewal from those teachers who have been my friends and allies through the years, the veterans like Frances Dukes and Mr. Bedrock and Ms. Gallombardo, but also from the young, impassioned, and excited teachers who are just beginning. This is why our correspondence and my visits to your classroom over the past year have meant so much to me. Even the visits in which every detail of the day did not go perfectly or when, on some occasions, I have managed to be no help to you at all and have even stirred your temporary wrath when I did something less than useful, even stupid, in your class, have nonetheless been happy memories.

I still recall the time I inadvertently messed up a lesson you were teaching about sentence structure. You had asked me to suggest a good short sentence and I didn't listen carefully and gave a sentence that went on and on forever. In front of all the children, you said that I hadn't paid attention and you thought I needed "a time-out." You made me go and sit down in the corner on the reading rug with that big floppy bear you let the children hold when they have misbehaved. I know I deserved this. I was grateful, though, when Dobie got up from his chair and brought me a decal of a frog to cheer me up.

I wanted to thank you at that moment for the patience and the playfulness with which you handled this. You said I'd acted "like a very, very foolish person—not like a grown-up man at all." But do you know I've seen you with your kids when you were being very foolish too? Thank goodness for that! I think that's one reason why they rush into your room so eagerly each morning. You said once, "My salary is pitiful, but I get paid in hugs." Thousands of other teachers who have all the normal problems, illnesses, and disappointments everybody has, but find that they forget these discontents the minute that they walk into their class each day, could say the same.

Some education students who want very much to teach in inner-city schools are given the impression, as I've noted, sometimes even by their own professors, that working in these kinds of schools will be a painful sacrifice—all struggle, but no joy. As I think you knew somehow before you even started out, it's not like that at all. At least, it shouldn't be. Even in the most adverse conditions, the work of a good teacher ought to be an act of stalwart celebration. It is in that sense of celebration, in my own belief at least, that teachers who have chosen out of love to work with children find their ultimate reward.

If there is a single message I wish I could pass on to young teachers and to people thinking about teaching, that would be the one. It's not political at all, not on the face of it; but fighting to defend that right to celebrate each perishable day and hour in a child's life may, in the current climate of opinion, be one of the greatest challenges we have.

P.S. As usual, one more thing that I forgot. I wanted to tell you what an absolutely fascinating, excellent and—to leave out no praise you deserve—super-terrific time I had last week when I was in your class. I'd forgotten all about green slime! Thank you for including me when you taught the children how to make it.

You told me, "Do not underestimate the economic value of producing slime successfully!" I'm going to repeat that someday when I'm at a conference of important CEOs. If they ask me how to make it, I'll be well prepared. "The consistency is what counts most," you said. I think I'll repeat that too.

As I promised, I'll be back on Monday.

EPILOGUE

Goodbye for Now

Dear Francesca,

This will be my final letter to you for a while. You'll be traveling with your sister for a good part of the summer, and I'm going to be traveling for several weeks as well.

Before I say goodbye for now, I hope that you will understand if I want to take this opportunity to say a few brief words about a recently departed friend who's given me more affirmation of my own ideas about the sensibilities and education of our children than any other grown-up I have known since I was a young teacher.

I suspect you know that I am thinking of Fred Rogers, since I've told you how important he became to me as a steadfast presence in my life during the ten years prior to his death and how hard it is to fully recognize, even to this day, that he is really gone.

I met Mr. Rogers late in 1992 when I was in Pittsburgh to be interviewed on the public television station in which Mr. Rogers' Neighborhood was taped. At the end of my interview, as the studio technicians were untangling the wire and the microphone they had attached to me, I heard a voice behind me calling me by my first name as if we already knew each other. There, only a couple feet away, looking exactly as he did on television except that his hair was turning gray, was Mr. Rogers.

He brought me into his studio and, at my request, showed me the closet where he put away his jacket at the start of every show, and then the setup for "The Neighborhood of Make-Believe" and, naturally, the trolley train, and he introduced me to the man who played the role of Mr. McFeely on the show, all of which impressed me every bit as much as I imagine it might have impressed a four- or five-year-old.

Then we sat down on his sofa for the first of many conversations we would have in years to come. He questioned me about my book Savage Inequalities, which I had published earlier that year, and he was so courteous and patient when I gave him rambling or awkward answers (I was at first a little nervous to be chatting suddenly with somebody whose mannerisms and whose face were so familiar to me) that I soon felt utterly at ease and no longer had that sense of something "just a bit unreal" that I usually feel in talking to a person who, to me, belongs within the borders of a TV screen.

From that point on, we spoke on the phone or corresponded with each other every month or so. We also managed to arrange things so that we could meet from time to time, once in Washington, the second time in New York City, where he asked if he could go with me to the South Bronx to meet the kids I wrote about. On that occasion, he asked me first if I thought his presence in the neighborhood might be "intimidating" to the children, a thought that never would have come into my mind. I teased him a little and replied, "I bet they can handle it!" So he said, "Okay! Then let's go to the Bronx!" When he asked me how I went there from Manhattan, I told him that the quickest way was by the Number 6 train to Brook Avenue. The idea of going on the subway seemed to please him very much.

The ride on the train, the visit to the elementary school where Mr. Bedrock and Ms. Dukes were teaching, the hours spent with children in the kindergarten classes, the visit we made later to the afterschool at St. Ann's Church, where Mario descended on him instantly (and wrapped his arms around his head and gave him a big kiss right in the middle of his forehead, then looked him in the eyes and told him, "Welcome to *my* neighborhood!")—all of this became imprinted on my memory as one of the most joyful days I ever spent in the South Bronx.

He later sent me photographs he took that day, assembled in an album with handwritten annotations next to pictures that held special meaning for him. Next to a picture of Mario, who was holding a stuffed animal beneath his arm, he wrote, "This one is my favorite." In subsequent months and years he kept on asking about Mario.

In retrospect, though, I think it was the teachers we had visited who were most affected by the time he spent with them. He squeezed himself into the kindergarten chairs so that he was at eye level with the children who surrounded him. He questioned them about their lives, or objects on their desks or in the room that were of interest to them, and he listened to their answers with his usual respectfulness and did not try to hurry them. He met with teachers in the older grades as well and asked them many questions about children in their classes. One thing that he didn't ask them was about the test scores of their pupils.

That visit took place in 1996. He made another visit with me to the neighborhood in autumn of 2000. As the momentum for intensive testing of young children and for scripted and didactic methods of instruction rapidly intensified during that period, he told me he had grown increasingly disturbed. The quiet way in which he spoke of his disconsolate reactions to this rising tide of what he viewed as an unnatural severity to children at a vulnerable moment in their lives reinforced my own beliefs more powerfully than any of the words or writings of the more specifically creden-tialed and established critics of these policies.

He also used to ask about my private life and would then return to something I had mentioned, maybe even six months after I had told it to him. For reasons that I didn't understand until a little later on, he grew especially attached to my dog, Sweetie Pie, who was a favorite of Pineapple too. (Pineapple couldn't figure out at first why Sweetie Pie was not al-lowed to fly with me, and sit in a seat beside me, when I took the shuttle to New York. When I ex-plained to her that the only way she could have come with me by plane was if I had put her in a box to travel in the baggage area and that I knew this would have frightened her, she insisted that I drive from Boston to the Bronx so Sweetie Pie could spend some time with her. Against all common sense—taking a five-hour drive with Sweetie Pie, two days in a row, involved a number of the misadventures you would probably expect—I finally complied.)

After Fred had seen a photograph of Sweetie Pie, he began to ask about her all the time and soon began to send her letters, usually for no particular occasion, but always on her birthdays. He would also call her on the phone at times and ask to speak to her and, when I put her floppy ear beside the phone, he'd talk to her, and she would sometimes give a good woof in reply.

He must have kept a careful calendar of birth-days of his friends because he never missed one of her birthdays and, if we were not at home, he always sang her "Happy Birthday" on my answering machine. He later told me she reminded him of his first dog, "whom," he said, "I loved beyond all measure. . . . I got her for taking terrible-tasting medicine when I was three. She lived until I was 21. You can imagine how I loved her."

A few years after that, when Sweetie Pie grew ill with a malignant tumor on her nose that pressed against her optic nerve and threatened to invade the bone around her brain, he asked me for repeated updates on the chemotherapy she had to undergo. At one point that fall, her right eye had to be removed and I hesitated for almost a month to tell Fred of her worsening condition. He wrote me a long and worried letter in which he said, "I hope your silence about Sweetie Pie doesn't mean the worst." It was, by then, the middle of December. He didn't mention in his letter that he too had recently been diagnosed with a malignancy. That letter about Sweetie Pie was the final message I received from him. Seven weeks later I read in The Boston Globe that he had died.

Francesca, I've mentioned the emphasis Mr. Rogers used to place on leaving open space and open time for children to express themselves and, when they do, the need for us to listen to them carefully. Now he's gone, and we are in an age of stern intentionality in which the possibilities for leaving open space and open times in which our children can reveal their secrets and unveil their souls have been diminished greatly in too many of our schools. The sacredness he saw in children has now been supplanted by more chastening concerns as to their future economic value, their "utility" and "productivity," words and ideas, as you can imagine, that he did not like at all.

Fred had studied theology as a young man, as I think I may have told you, and had been ordained in the Presbyterian denomination with "a ministry to children." But he also identified with children in a manner more intrinsic to his personality than that which is perhaps suggested by a word like "ministry." He wrote a song in the last year of his life, one he never had a chance to finish, that he called, "The Child Who's in Me Still, and Sometimes Not So Still!" I love that title. It reminds me of the look of sheer exhilaration on his face when we were riding to the South Bronx on the New York subway. He seemed as excited as a young boy might have been by all the lights and noises and the people coming through the train to sell CDs and flashlight batteries and those many other items that are sold, illegally perhaps, for bargain prices to the passengers.

That song inevitably makes me think, as well, of all those easily exhilarated and impulsive first-year teachers that I meet and many older teachers too who have never wholly given up the child in themselves and might not be nearly as good teachers if they ever did. I look to those teachers to hold to their hearts the legacy that Mr. Rogers left us. It's a fragile legacy because, although he was immersed in Eriksonian ideals and had studied with Erikson scholars and, of course, knew Erikson himself, nothing about his way of listening to children or *being* with young children is considered "research-based" or "scientific," which are the code words of acceptability these days, as you know all too well.

Mr. Rogers' legacy is viewed as "soft" and "too impressionistic" in an age when very hard and measurable outcomes have been stringently demanded by the overseers of public education, whose certitude about the practices that they enforce seems nearly absolute. I pray that teachers of all ages will reject the cheap rewards of overstated absolutes and honor instead the self-effacing virtues of the kindest man and wisest friend of children we may have the opportunity to know for many years.

As I've said, Francesca, I'll be leaving soon for meetings that will keep me far from Boston for a while. During the weeks when I'm away, I'm afraid I'll be caught up for more time than I'd like in some of the heated issues you and I have been discussing over the past year.

I don't mean that I regret the opportunity to stand up and say what I believe about these issues, even though, as I have said, I *don't* especially enjoy the part that's adversarial. I simply mean I'll miss the times when I've been able to sit in on classes like your own with no particular agenda on my mind other than to get to know the children in the same way that their teachers do, and talk with them, and help them some-times with their work whenever teachers like you make this possible.

I'll miss the mysteries of little ones like Dobie who stuff sugar in their pockets or the friendly girl I got to know last year at another school in Boston who be-came so terribly excited by the fact that I was wearing brand-new sneakers, blue ones, the flat oldfashioned kind you know I like, which struck her as incredibly amazing because, as she whispered to me very heat-edly and secretly, "My little brother has exactly the same sneakers!" Then, in keeping with her wish to be precise: "Only his are red instead of blue. . . ."

Here's all I really mean by this: In the midst of the forensics and the sometimes fierce encounters tak-ing place in the political arena, I always miss and never forget the real life of the classroom and the real work of the teacher: the lessons to plan, the timelines to be drawn, the "Good Morning" messages to be dis-played across the board, the students to be comforted, instructed, and empowered to take satisfaction in the act of learning while they also gain, as much as possi-ble, the critical capacities to challenge misimpressions or misinformation that do not sound "right" to them or which they suspect to be "not true."

To you, Francesca, and to all the other energized and hopeful younger teachers who will follow after you during the years to come, I'd like to end by saying that I pray you'll never lose the sense of joy and tenderness that brings good people to the task of teaching in the first place. I wish you years of happiness among your children, plenty of hugs and lots of foolishness, many caterpillars, snails, and other interesting things that creep and crawl, unhurried hours of unfolding treasures for your children on the reading rug and helping all the little pipers you may meet to overcome their furies just enough to learn their lessons, channel their passions into patterns that may rescue them from needless times of suffering when they get into higher grades of school, and, for at least a couple of hours every day, to stay connected to their chairs!

And, when it is needed, I also wish you rightful anger, vigorous denunciation, and the saving grace of sly irreverence and the skillful uses of ironical detachment from the soul-destroying practices and terminologies of experts who are positive they know "what works" within the unjust and unequal system they no longer choose to challenge or denounce but who seem to know only too little of the hearts of children. Resist the deadwood of predictability. Embrace the unexpected. Revel in the run-on sentences. Celebrate silliness. Dig deep into the world of whim. Sprinkle your children's lives, no matter how difficult many of those lives may be, with hundreds of brightly colored seeds of jubilation. Enjoy the wild flowers!

Thank you, Francesca, for teaching me far more than I have ever taught to you. I'll be looking forward to a good reunion with your very grown-up second graders once I'm back from all this traveling next fall. Meanwhile, have a wonderful summer and if you should happen to see any of the kids before you leave, tell them please that I send lots of love.

Also to you!

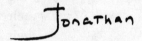

AFTERWORD

A Retrospective Conversation
with Francesca

In looking through these letters as I have assembled them for publication here, Francesca tells me they bring back a wave of other memories of happy details from her year of teaching first grade in the Boston schools, before she was promoted with her students to the second grade and, in the next year, as it turned out, to the third. And she keeps on recollecting incidents and snippets of good conversations with the children that she wishes she had told me in the months when I was visiting her class and we were writing back and forth to one another. If I tried to tuck in all these lovely moments that I missed, this Afterword might go on for another 50 pages.

The one request she makes to me, however, that I know holds high importance to her now, in retrospect, is that I make very clear to future teachers that her first year in the classroom was not always a self-confident and worry-free experience, as some of these letters may imply, but that she underwent the same self-questionings and disappointments that most teachers at the start of their careers almost inevitably undergo.

Perhaps, in writing these letters, I was so impressed by her high-spirited demeanor and her seemingly unshakable good humor and her skillful ways of dealing with resistance on the part of Dobie and some of the other children in her class, that I didn't pick up on the moments of self-doubt to which she now refers.

One of those moments, as she recollects, came at a time while I was traveling in the mid-winter, when she says she felt a sudden wave of great concern about what she believed to be her students' lack of gains in reading skills or, at least, their failure to achieve those rapid gains that she had hopefully anticipated. A particularly dark and dreary time in January—rain and slush instead of clean and cheerful snow—added to the grimness of the mood that settled in upon her for a while.

Then, to make things even worse, she tells me that she had an awful confrontation with a mother who was furious about the first report card that her child had received, in which Francesca noted that the little girl had stopped doing her homework and was coming late to class. She asked her mother if there might be reasons for this change in her behavior that would help Francesca compensate in any way at school.

It happened that this child was one of the nicest and most bashful children in the room, "a little dreamer," as Francesca says, "who used to go off in her private spaceship now and then" but soon "came sailing back into her chair" with a contented-looking smile on her face. I used to see her sidle up beside

Francesca quietly while she was teaching and just stand and gaze at her with patience while she waited for the hug that she expected. "She doesn't have a mean bone in her body," says Francesca. "I had to be strict with her to make her do her work, but I think she knew that I adored her."

Her mother, moreover, had been so friendly to Francesca up until that time that her suddenly explosive manner seemed incomprehensible at first. "She used to be so nice to me! Then, the very next day after I had given out report cards, she charged into the school and stormed right through the building and began to scream at me and followed me into the classroom, and she cursed me out in front of all the children."

Francesca's principal told her that the child's mother had been going through a bad time in her private life during that period. The report card may have struck her as simply the final blow. And it also may have been a confirmation to her that the troubles in her own life had been having more of an effect upon her child than she'd realized, which is not the kind of news a mother likes to find out from her child's teacher.

But Francesca says she worried also that the way she'd posed the question about what might possibly be going on within the child's life at home may have sounded too invasive and abrupt. Since she'd never had to speak of serious problems with this child in the past, she told herself she should have raised this issue in a good unhurried conversation with the mother, not in a report card. She says she chided herself for having handled this ineptly.

But it was the reading difficulties of her students that disturbed her most, she says, because she truly had believed the methods of instruction she'd been using—lots of writing, and immersion in a rich array of children's books, and small-group phonics sessions when she felt that they were needed—were planting the seeds that ought to have begun to sprout and blossom by this time. Suddenly now, as she recalls, a vague uneasiness about her own convictions overcame her.

After turning for advice to a reading specialist and literacy coach who spent three days a week within her school, and after stiffening her lessons in skill-building just enough to guarantee more continuity from one day to the next, she found her students moving ahead more rapidly, although she says her worries did not wholly dissipate until the reading specialist assured her, maybe a month later, that her class was keeping pace with children in the other first grade at the school, whose teacher was a great deal more experienced.

Still, she says, "I went through a time when I felt very vulnerable, and fallible, and I think you need to make this clear because all teachers will go through these periods of insecurity, and they'll recognize when they have made mistakes and temporarily may lose their confidence. If you leave this out, it gives the incorrect impression that I was, right from the starting gate, one of those 'super-teachers' that we used to joke about who allegedly turn everything they touch to gold. We both know that that wasn't so. It's *never* so. And I think beginning teachers need to know this, so they won't berate themselves too much when things go wrong but will accept their imperfections, take a little time to rethink what they have been doing, then move on. . . ."

I think the truth of the matter is that I respected so much what Francesca tried to do within that classroom, and did so well for somebody so young and new to her profession, that I may have been a bit too hesitant about expressing observations that might have discouraged her. Then, too, because I get distracted easily by the words and personalities of children when I'm in a public school, I simply may have missed some of those feelings of self-questioning that she experienced.

Francesca always seemed to me to move among the children in her classroom with a special kind of dignity, serenity, and pride. The dignity was in her character. The pride was in her children, in their intellectual and personal development, and in the ways in which they learned to be kind and supportive to each other. The intermittent worries that she felt may have been masked beneath that surface of serenity. She wanted the classroom to be happy for her children and she did not want them to be burdened with a recognition of her own anxieties. I suspect they must have sensed those moments anyway. I think they must have recognized when she was feeling sad or insecure, because they were so fond of her and studied her so closely. But I also think that teachers will be grateful for her honesty.

APPENDIX I

Recipe for Green Slime

Francesca said, "Do not underestimate the economic value of producing slime successfully!" There
is, unfortunately, nothing helpful on this subject in No
Child Left Behind. So, with Francesca's help, I've tried
to fill the vacuum here. In order to be certain this is
research-based and scientific, I have relied on two practitioners, the first of whom is Patricia Jensen, whose
website posting "Slime Recipe Favorites" indicates that
there are both easy and more difficult recipes for slime.
Following is my adaptation of her recipe for "Easy
Slime":

INGREDIENTS
$^1/_4$ cup of white glue
$1^1/_4$ cups of water
1 tablespoon of Borax
green food coloring (if that's your preference)

INSTRUCTIONS
Add the Borax to a cup of warm water.
Stir until the Borax is dissolved.

Make a half-water, half-white glue solution by
    taking $1/4$ cup of each and mixing thoroughly.
In a plastic bag, add equal portions of the Borax
    solution and the white glue solution.
Add a few drops of green food coloring.
Seal the bag and knead the mixture.
Open the bag. You have made green slime.

The second source of information I've relied upon is provided by a science teacher, Peggy Ashbrook, in an article entitled "Nurturing Young Chemists," published in a magazine called Science and Children (February 2006).

"More than just 'fun,' " she writes, "making slime is a great opportunity to introduce young children to safe laboratory practices and teach them how to follow a procedure." Another reason why this is a good activity for children is that there is "wiggle room" in "the measurements of substances."

Before combining substances, she says, "discuss the properties of each material." Ask children: "What do you think would happen if we mixed these substances together?"

After students mix the Borax solution with the white glue solution and knead the mixture with their hands and then remove it from the plastic bag, they will discover that the mixture they have made is no longer "a slimy goop" but has been transformed into "a stretchy polymer" of a consistency that is "somewhere between the result of a forceful sneeze and a superball."

"All students," she points out, "must wear safety goggles." They should also be reminded not to eat the Borax or the glue. . . .

Francesca advises me that her students found additional, but less scientific, information in a book entitled Bartholomew and the Oobleck, by Theodor Geisel, better known as Dr. Seuss. All teachers, she adds, do not insist on pupils wearing goggles, but reminding children not to eat the Borax is of the greatest possible importance. "Teachers who neglect to emphasize this point run the risk of being fired," she observes, "and they probably deserve to be. Don't expect the parents to defend you if their children eat the Borax!"

Francesca and I hope this information will be useful to our friends of every age.

APPENDIX II

Leads and Contacts

To obtain updated information on the issues I have been addressing in these letters to Francesca, readers are invited to contact me and those who work with me at the following address:

Education Action!
16 Lowell Street
Cambridge, Massachusetts 02138
www.edaction.com
educationactioninfo@gmail.com

Education Action! (the exclamation point is part of our name) is primarily a movement-building organization dedicated to the goal of achieving equal opportunity and racially desegregated classrooms in our public schools. But we also do our best to respond to the daily challenges educators face in dealing with high-stakes exams, scripted instructional materials, and other aspects of the new accountability regimes imposed on teachers by the federal government and by local boards of education.

Another source of information readers will find useful is an experienced and dynamic organization called Rethinking Schools, which publishes a widely circulated magazine of the same name but also keeps close watch on teacher groups in various communities and periodically updates their status and the ways to reach them.

Those who would like to plug into the database of Rethinking Schools should get in touch with its editors directly. Along with its contact lists and the magazine itself, which is by far the most important publication for politically resistant teachers (and the only one I know that's written mostly by schoolteachers), Rethinking Schools also produces valuable materials that speak directly to the issues raised within this book. I recommend especially "Rethinking Our Classrooms: Teaching for Equity and Justice" (Volumes I and II), "Selling Out Our Schools: Vouchers, Markets, and the Future of Public Education," and a very useful handbook, "The New Teacher Book," written exclusively by teachers.

The website for Rethinking Schools—both the organization and the publication—is the following:

www.rethinkingschools.org

The mail address is:

Rethinking Schools
1001 East Keefe Avenue
Milwaukee, Wisconsin 53212

I hope that readers of this book who are looking for a sense of solidarity in what is frequently the lonely work of seeking justice in our public schools will find these contacts helpful.

ACKNOWLEDGMENTS

Among those who have helped me most in editing these letters, I want to begin by thanking my beloved friend Tisha Graham, who has painstakingly reviewed every book I've written since we started working with each other in the 1970s when Tisha was my first research assistant. I also thank my close political colleague Cassie Schwerner, who began her work in education policy by researching and editing Savage Inequalities and Amazing Grace and who has continued to look with an eagle eye at every word I've published since. Both she and Tisha scrutinized this book for accuracy and for the inevitable repetitions that pop up in letters written sometimes many months apart, and also helped me to correct my memories of past events on those occasions when, in writing to Francesca, I may have blithely cruised right past a point that they lived through with me and therefore remember vividly.

I'm especially indebted to Bob Peterson, one of the founders and the initial editor of Rethinking Schools. Bob and I keep in close contact with each other, and this was particularly the case during the year when I was corresponding with Francesca and visiting her school. I think that his compassionate approach to younger teachers and his long experience in teaching in Milwaukee may have helped to make some of my answers to Francesca of more practical assistance to her than they might otherwise have been.

I also thank Jan Resseger, a lay minister in the United Church of Christ who is also the chairperson of the Committee on Public Education at the National Council of Churches. Jan has reviewed these letters carefully and corrected factual mistakes; but, most important, she has helped to reinforce my views about the necessary role in the defense of public schools, and in combating segregated and unequal education, that can, and must, be taken by progressive forces in our national religious life. For this, I am most grateful.

In the production of this book, I owe the greatest debt to Amy Ehntholt, who has taken precious time from the demanding work required by her doctoral studies in the classics to enable me to turn my messy and handwritten letters into a completed text. For the difficult task of checking and confirming factual matters that are in the public record (a maddening job when she was trying to get through the multiple layers of assistants-to-assistants that surround so many of the knowledgeable people I asked her to reach), I am grateful to my executive assistant, Nayad Abrahamian. Nayad, who is also one of the chief organizers of our network of progressive teachers, is one of those impassioned souls who, I am convinced, will carry on this struggle long after I and those with whom I've worked these many years are no longer here to fan the flames of discontent.

I feel very fortunate to have had an empathetic and supportive editor, Lucinda Bartley, and a loyal publisher, Steve Ross, who have been more patient with me than I have had any reason to expect. I am a pain in the neck for editors and publishers. I'm glad that Crown puts up with me.

Finally, I can't think of any way to adequately thank Francesca. She is, of course, the spirit of this book, a gloriously talented and unselfish woman and, for me, a symbol of the best that we should look for in the teachers of our children. I hope a future generation of young teachers will, by their courage and excitement and tenacity, give her the only thanks that I suspect she'd really like.

NOTES

Among my previous books to which reference is made in my letters to Francesca are the following:

Death at an Early Age (Houghton Mifflin, 1967)

Rachel and Her Children (Crown, 1988)

Savage Inequalities (Crown, 1991)

Amazing Grace (Crown, 1995)

Ordinary Resurrections (Crown, 2000)

The Shame of the Nation (Crown, 2005)

All of these books are now available in paperback editions: *Death at an Early Age* from New American Library, *Rachel and Her Children* and *The Shame of the Nation* from Three Rivers Press, all the others from Harper Perennial.

small pin on my lapel, an "equal" sign, white parallel lines on a black background, that was commonly worn during those days in symbolic solidarity with freedom workers in the South. "It's a nice pin," she said, "but don't wear it here. . . . You never know when it could be misunderstood."

CHAPTER FOUR: TEACHING THE YOUNG, BUT LEARNING FROM THE OLD

34, 35   SOUTH BRONX TEACHERS FRANCES DUKES AND LOUIS BEDROCK: For descriptions of their classes and their teaching practices, see *Ordinary Resurrections* and *The Shame of the Nation*.

40   SUBURBAN ELEMENTARY SCHOOL IN WHICH INTERDISTRICT INTEGRATION HAD RECENTLY BEGUN: The program, known as METCO, began in 1966 and now encompasses nearly three dozen Boston suburbs. See Notes for pp. 187 and 188.

42   "TO REMEMBER LIKE THE OLD AND BE HONEST LIKE CHILDREN": "In Memory of Sigmund Freud," *Selected Poems W. H. Auden* (New York: Vintage Books, 1979).

CHAPTER FIVE: WILD FLOWERS

45   "YOUNG CHILDREN GIVE US GLIMPSES OF SOME THINGS THAT ARE ETERNAL": Fred Rogers, in conversation with me, June 1998.

46, 47   ARIEL'S POETRY AND THAT OF OTHER CHILDREN IN HER CLASS: Ariel's school, P.S. 30, was at the time one of the more progressive and more successful elementary schools in the South Bronx.

48, 49   "FIVE ESSENTIAL ELEMENTS" OF A GOOD WALL DISPLAY: The talented teacher at P.S. 65, Christina Young, who refused to doctor writings by her pupils, and who became disheartened by the proto-military test-prep regimen, quit the school a year later and gave up education altogether.

54   "I AM PROFICIENT IN CONSIDERING THE SIX TRAITS OF EFFECTIVE WRITING": I copied this from the wall of a fifth grade classroom at Seattle's Thurgood Marshall School in the fall of 2003. See pp. 160 and 161 and Notes for these pages.

CHAPTER SIX: THE LITTLE PIPER

59, 60   THE PIPER WHO FELL ASLEEP DURING A TIME OF PLAGUE: *A Journal of the Plague Year,* by Daniel Defoe, originally published in 1772 and cited here from the Penguin Classics edition (New York: Penguin Books, 1986).

60, 61   CHILDREN IN HOMELESS SHELTER IN NEW YORK: The conditions in this shelter are described in my book *Rachel and Her Children.*

70   "NOBODY LOVES A GENIUS CHILD": The lines are from Langston Hughes' poem "Genius Child." See *The Collected Poems of Langston Hughes* (New York: Vintage Classics, 1995).

CHAPTER SEVEN: THE USES OF "DIVERSITY"

74   NEWSPAPERS AVOID TERM "RACIAL SEGREGATION" IN DESCRIBING SEGREGATED SCHOOLS: Notable exceptions are the *St. Louis Post-Dispatch* and *Newsday,* both of which have written with consistent candor about segregated schooling in their own communities.

"CHILDREN FROM DIVERSE BACKGROUNDS" AT KANSAS CITY SCHOOL WHERE 99.6 PERCENT OF STUDENTS ARE BLACK: J. S. Chick Elementary School, Kansas City, Missouri. See Annual Reporting of Information by School Districts, Missouri Department of Elementary and Secondary Education, 2004.

74, 75   "DIVERSITY" OF STUDENT POPULATION IN NEW YORK DISTRICT WHERE ALL BUT FOUR OF 2,800 STUDENTS ARE BLACK OR HISPANIC: Roosevelt Public Schools. See School Report for Roosevelt district (New York State Education Department, 2001–2002) and "The Roosevelt UFSD 21st Century Community Learning Centers Program," Roosevelt Public Schools, 2001–2002.

77   INCREASE IN SEGREGATION OF BLACK STUDENTS NATIONALLY AND STATISTICS FOR NEW YORK AND CALIFORNIA: All of this is extensively documented in *The Shame of the Nation,* based upon data provided by Professor Gary Orfield and his colleagues at the Civil Rights Project, Harvard University, in 2004 and 2005.

77, 78   NUMBER OF WHITE CHILDREN AT P.S. 65 AND IN THE SURROUNDING DISTRICT: Annual School Reports for P.S. 65,

New York City Public Schools, 1997 to 2002, and "Keeping Track of New York City's Children," Citizens' Committee for Children of New York, 1997.

79 RACIAL SEGREGATION OF MARTIN LUTHER KING, JR. HIGH SCHOOL IN MIDTOWN MANHATTAN: Annual School Report, New York City Public Schools, 2001–2002.

CHAPTER EIGHT: BEWARE THE JARGON FACTORY

88 "A TEXT-TO-SELF CONNECTION": The highly respected literacy specialist Lucy Calkins, who is identified, more perhaps than any other academic scholar, with the teaching practice known as "balanced literacy," uses this phrase and others like it in explaining to teachers practical ways in which to organize their lessons. What was offensive to Francesca was not the terminology itself (she and I are both admirers of Professor Calkins) but the patronizing statement of the "meta-lady" that she would not understand something that she had clearly recognized already unless she was willing to perceive it in these formalized and hyphenated terms. "The ossification of these words and categories," Calkins has herself observed, "can get in the way of using language for authentic purposes." (Interview with Professor Calkins at Teachers College in New York, 2004.)

91 FORMER U.S. EDUCATION SECRETARY LAURO CAVAZOS CITED: *New Republic,* July 10, 1989.
  "WHAT IS SCHOOL RESTRUCTURING?": "Task Force on High School Restructuring, Final Report," Kentucky Department of Education, June 30, 1993.

93 "SUNDAY-AFTERNOON NEUROSIS": Paul Goodman is quoted from the paperback revision of his 1956 book *Growing Up Absurd* (New York: Vintage Books, 1960).

93*ff* THE "EFFICACY" MAN: Variants of this term have been employed for years. In New York City, in the 1960s, there was a government-sponsored program called "Effective Schools," which was unsuccessful, and, a few years later, a program known as "More Effective Schools," which also turned out to be unsuccessful. By the 1970s, "efficacy" had emerged as the term of choice. There is today an Efficacy Institute which, according to its website in 2006, states that its model is "based on the idea that intelligence can be built through

Effective Effort." The "Efficacy Seminar" teaches "Efficacy concepts and principles," and delivers additional services such as "Applied Efficacy." The "Efficacy Model," according to the website, "symbolizes the Process of Development . . . where success increases confidence and effort leading to even more success, and so on." Francesca does not know if the "Efficacy Man" who visited her school and shut her down abusively when she asked a question was affiliated with the Efficacy Institute or another organization that employs some of the same vocabulary.

CHAPTER NINE: AESTHETIC MERRIMENT

100*ff* APRIL GAMBLE'S THIRD GRADE CLASSROOM IN THE BRONX: In writing to Francesca, I relied on the description of this classroom in my book *Ordinary Resurrections*.

104 THE VERY HUNGRY CATERPILLAR, BY ERIC CARLE: New York: Philomel Books, 1987.

105 MISSION STATEMENT ABOUT "GLOBAL MARKETPLACE": These business-driven mission statements (in another classroom, this one in Hartford, Connecticut, one of the stated missions of the school was "to develop productive citizens" for "successful global competition") are seen frequently in inner-city schools, almost never in the suburbs.

108 INTENTION OF BUSH ADMINISTRATION "TO CHANGE THE FACE OF READING INSTRUCTION . . . FROM AN ART TO A SCIENCE": Susan B. Neuman, Assistant Secretary for Elementary and Secondary Education, U.S. Department of Education, cited in *New York Times,* January 9, 2002.

108, 109 "HOW TO BE AN ARTIST" AND "I LIKE TO MIX IT UP": My question to the teacher had to do, specifically, with a familiar form of book exposure known as "guided reading," where the books are usually sorted by the levels of ability it requires to read them. The teacher said she deviated from this practice on a random basis now and then and let the children choose their books according to a topic that excited them. In saying that she liked "to mix it up," she explained that she and her fellow-teachers made these and other variations, in at least some part, in order to maintain their own enthusiasm and not find themselves stuck in a rut of enervating by-the-book predictability. The teacher and her classroom in Durham, North Carolina, are described in further detail in *The Shame of the Nation*.

CHAPTER TEN: HIGH-STAKES TESTS AND OTHER MODERN MISERIES

112*ff*   TEST-DRILLING, CANCELLATION OF RECESS, TESTING OF KINDERGARTEN CHILDREN, DENIAL OF NAP TIME, OTHER OBSERVATIONS ABOUT TESTING: Much of this information is documented in *The Shame of the Nation*. For Atlanta's abolition of recess and its intentional construction of schools without playgrounds since state testing pressures grew severe in the middle and late 1990s, see *Atlanta Journal-Constitution,* April 14, 1998, and September 21, 2006, and *New York Times,* April 7, 1998. For Chicago's virtual abolition of recess, see *Chicago Tribune,* October 23, 2006, which notes, for example, that a principal at one elementary school "allows pupils out to play after lunch only in the spring—after they finish the state tests that determine the school's progress under No Child Left Behind." In Chicago, according to *Catalyst Chicago,* October 2006, "fewer than one in five schools . . . provides daily scheduled recess for all kids, and only about one in 16 . . . provides for a recess of at least 20 minutes. . . . Typically, schools with more low-income students are less likely to offer recess. . . ."

114   "KEEP GOING. THE WHOLE PAGE. ALL BY YOURSELF": Cited from a kindergarten teacher in Santa Paula, California, in *Los Angeles Times,* October 6, 2001.

"KINDERGARTEN IS NOT LIKE IT USED TO BE": Alabama school official cited in *Atlanta Journal-Constitution,* October 3, 2003. "Playtime in kindergarten," notes education writer Clara Hemphill (*New York Times,* July 26, 2006), "is giving way to worksheets, math drills and fill-in-the-bubble standardized exams." At a Brooklyn charter school named Achievement First, part of a network of such charter schools, she notes, "there is no time for . . . naps or recess. There is homework every night. For much of the day, the children are asked to sit quietly with their hands folded as their teachers drill them. . . ." Pressures like these "can be especially intense in poorer neighborhoods" where schools are "struggling to meet the demands of the federal law known as No Child Left Behind. . . ."

115 NEARLY A MILLION OF OUR POOREST THREE-TO-FIVE-YEAR-OLDS PRESENTLY EXCLUDED FROM FEDERAL HEAD START PROGRAM: Interview with Yasmine Daniel, director of Early Childhood Department at the Children's Defense Fund, October 2006. According to the Children's Defense Fund, only 845,000 three-to-five-year-olds are now enrolled in Head Start. At the average per-pupil cost of $7,200 for a year of Head Start, an added federal allocation of about $7 billion yearly would enable almost every eligible child now excluded to benefit from Head Start for at least one year.

"UNIVERSAL PRE-K" IN NEW YORK STATE: *Education Week,* April 9, 2003; *New York Times,* February 2, 2003. New York, at least, makes an effort in the right direction. In my state of Massachusetts, in comparison, former Governor Mitt Romney vetoed legislation that would have made preschool universal. According to *The Boston Globe* (August 17, 2006), Mr. Romney stated "that the value of universal preschool is unproven." The *Globe* notes that only "about 15 percent of Massachusetts four-year-olds are served by the federal Head Start program or the state-funded prekindergarten program, both of which target the state's neediest children."

"THE BABY IVIES": Tuition for these exclusive New York City preschools is documented in *The Shame of the Nation.*

119 "THE STUDENT WILL PRODUCE A NARRATIVE PROCEDURE": The teacher had copied this nearly verbatim from a document called "Performance Standards: English Language Arts . . . ," New York City Public Schools, 1997.

120 SCRIPTED LESSONS, USED PRIMARILY IN INNER-CITY SCHOOLS: For a defense of one of the most draconian of these scripted programs, known as "Success for All" (this is the system I observed at Pineapple's school in the South Bronx), and my reply to this defense, see *Phi Delta Kappan,* April 2006.

122 PERSISTENT GULF IN LITERACY LEVELS BETWEEN MINORITY AND WHITE CHILDREN AND COMPARISON OF BLACK TWELFTH GRADERS TO WHITE SEVENTH GRADERS: *Education Week,* November 3, 2004. The director of the Washington-based Education Trust notes in this article that the achievement

gaps between white and minority children have "widened
. . . on our watch."

70 PERCENT OF BLACK MALES IN NEW YORK CITY AND CHI-
CAGO FAIL TO GRADUATE IN FOUR YEARS: *Education Week,*
December 1, 2004. New York City has, for many years, disguised its dropout rate by concealing many of its dropouts
in a separate category known as "discharged" students. (For
documentation of this statistical subterfuge, see *Ordinary
Resurrections* and *The Shame of the Nation.*) In the class of
2005, for instance, nearly 23 percent of students were described as "discharged" and, for this reason, not included in
the city's drop-out figures. Even without including so-called
discharged students, the city reported a drop-out rate of 42
percent (*New York Post,* November 24, 2006). Similar patterns of understated drop-out rates have been thoroughly
documented in Houston and Chicago. (See *The Shame of the
Nation.*)

APPLICATION OF B. F. SKINNER'S WORK IN RAT PSYCHOLOGY
AND STIMULUS-RESPONSE TO THE EDUCATION OF CHILDREN:
For Skinner's exposition of his views in this regard, see
About Behaviorism, by B. F. Skinner (New York: Random
House, 1974).

123 PRECIPITOUS DECLINE IN ADMISSIONS OF BLACK STUDENTS
TO STUYVESANT HIGH SCHOOL IN NEW YORK: *New York
Times,* March 18 and August 4, 1995, and August 18, 2006.

124 TESTING ADVOCATES CLAIM THAT HIGH-STAKES TESTS EN-
ABLE TEACHERS TO ADDRESS SPECIFIC WEAKNESSES OF STU-
DENTS: "Teachers can use this new information," said former
U.S. Secretary of Education Roderick Paige, "to tailor in-
struction to meet every child's needs." (U.S. Department of
Education, March 10, 2004.)

125 DELAYS IN RECEIVING THE RESULTS OF HIGH-STAKES TESTS:
In New York City, to give a recent example, "the results of
the standardized reading and math exams" given in grades
three through eight in January and March 2006 were not
available until September, noted the (New York) *Daily News*
(August 31, 2006). Additional delays and mass confusion
have occurred when major testing companies mis-score exams, as they do repeatedly. Errors in the scoring of standardized exams have led some districts to require kids to
go to "test-prep summer school," as was the case last year
in New York City (*New York Post,* September 24, 2006), in

order to escape the risk of nonpromotion. In other states, merit pay to teachers who allegedly had raised the scores of students had already been awarded when it was discovered that the tests had been mis-scored. According to "How Test Companies Fail Your Kids," in *Bloomberg Markets,* December 2006, McGraw-Hill's testing affiliate "hired temporary workers who couldn't spell to score tests," while Harcourt Assessment, which "is making the most errors," gave inflated scores to thousands of students in Nevada after producing tests "with missing pages . . . and flawed instructions." In all, Harcourt has given children incorrect scores in at least 15 states. These and other testing companies, *Bloomberg Markets* notes, "generated $2.8 billion in revenue from testing and test preparation" in 2005.

CHAPTER ELEVEN: THE SINGLE WORST, MOST DANGEROUS IDEA

131 HIGH-STAKES TESTING AS A "SHAMING RITUAL": "They put us in a statistical deathtrap by imposing on us standards that are impossible to meet," says David Engle, the respected former principal of Seattle's Ballard High. "I've believed from the beginning that this was intended to discredit public education, to convince the nation that 'the system's broken,' as they like to say, and to pave the way for private-sector forces to move in and take apart the public system, school by school, when test scores don't rise fast enough to come up to the arbitrary le﹘ is they demand." (Interview with Engle, Washington ﹘.﹘., December 2006.)

132, 133 "WEALTHY PEOPLE HAVE THESE CHOICES . . . WHY, THEN, SHOULDN'T YOU ENJOY THEM TOO?": Former U.S. Secretary of Education and now U.S. Senator Lamar Alexander made this argument on public television in a debate with me and other educators in 1991. "The people in America who do not have choice are poor people," Mr. Alexander said. "I have choice. I can . . . send my child to a public or private school. A poor person cannot do that. . . . Choice gives to disadvantaged Americans the same opportunities that better-off Americans have." (MacNeil/Lehrer *NewsHour,* April 18, 1991.)

136, 137 VOUCHER ADVOCATE JOHN CHUBB CITED ON DECISION-MAKING SKILLS OF LOW-INCOME PARENTS: *New York Times,*

August 22, 1990. Mr. Chubb, "a founding partner, executive vice-president, and chief education officer of Edison Schools," a for-profit private education company, is also "a distinguished visiting fellow" at the conservative Hoover Institution and "a nonresident senior fellow at the Brookings Institution," according to a biography prepared by the Hoover Institution and given to my assistant, Nayad Abrahamian, in October 2006 by Mr. Chubb's office at the New York City headquarters of Edison Schools.

137, 138   MR. CHUBB CITED IN MORE CANDID TERMS: "No School Is An Island," *Brookings Review,* Fall 1986, reprinted in *The Politics of Excellence and Choice in Education,* ed. by William Boyd and Charles Kerchner (New York: The Falmer Press, 1988); *Politics, Markets, and America's Schools* (Washington, D.C.: The Brookings Institution, 1990); "Educational Choice," *Wisconsin Policy Research Institute Report,* March 1989. The book and the two cited articles were co-authored with political scientist Terry Moe.

139, 140   ANALYSTS AT MONTGOMERY SECURITIES CITED: "The Emerging Investment Opportunity in Education," by Michael Moe and R. Keith Gay of Montgomery Securities, San Francisco, undated.

"THE K−12 MARKET IS THE BIG ENCHILADA": Michael Moe, cited in *Education Industry Report,* December 1998.

141   VOUCHERS HISTORICALLY IDENTIFIED WITH SEGREGATIONIST INTERESTS: In 1956, white parents in Virginia "established the first publicly funded school vouchers in the United States . . . for the explicit purpose of circumventing the historic *Brown* desegregation decision," note education writers Bob Peterson and Barbara Miner. "Eventually, the Virginia program and similar plans passed by segregationist southern legislatures in the 1950s were ruled unconstitutional." (*Colorlines,* Spring 1999.)

144   THE BELL CURVE, CO-AUTHORED BY CHARLES MURRAY: Murray is generally believed to be the primary author of this work (New York: Free Press, 1994). His co-author was the late Richard Herrnstein. Murray's earlier work, *Losing Ground* (New York: Basic Books, 1984), made a carefully developed argument for privatizing inner-city education as a subset of his larger argument for ending or limiting social benefits to poor parents and their children.

THE "NATURAL RESULTS": The phrase appears in Murray's

essay "Helping the Poor: A Few Modest Proposals" (*Commentary,* May 1985), in which he expands upon his arguments in *Losing Ground.*

"SOME PEOPLE ARE BETTER THAN OTHERS": This is the passage in *Losing Ground* in which Murray writes these words, not exclusively in reference to vouchers but in reference to the full sweep of governmental policies he believes this nation should adopt in its treatment of poor people: "Some people are better than others. They deserve more of society's rewards. . . . A principal function of social policy is to make sure they have the opportunity to reap those rewards. Government cannot identify the worthy, but it can protect a society in which the worthy can identify themselves. . . . I am proposing triage of a sort, triage by self-selection. In triage on the battlefield, the doctor makes the decision— this one gets treatment, that one waits, the other one is made comfortable while waiting to die. In our social triage, the decision is left up to the patient. . . . The patient always has the right to fail. Society always has the right to let him."

CHAPTER TWELVE: IT IS EVIL TO TELL LIES TO CHILDREN

151 "TELLING LIES TO THE YOUNG IS WRONG": The poem by Yevgeny Yevtushenko, which is entitled "Lies," is translated from the Russian by Robin Milner-Gulland. See *Yevtushenko: Selected Poems* (New York: Dutton, 1962).

LIES MY TEACHER TOLD ME: The book of that title, written by James Loewen (New York: Simon and Schuster, 1995), bears the subtitle "Everything Your American History Textbook Got Wrong."

153 OHIO GOVERNOR AND LEGISLATURE RESIST REPEATED COURT DETERMINATIONS THAT SCHOOL FINANCE SYSTEM VIOLATES STATE CONSTITUTION: The legal action, *DeRolph v. State,* filed in 1991, led to three successive decisions (1997, 2000, 2001) in which the state's supreme court found the state in violation of Ohio's constitution. A fourth decision, in which a more conservative court, elected with the political backing of the governor, ruled again (2002) that the system of school finance was unconstitutional but simultaneously stated that

NOTES

the court was formally releasing jurisdiction in the case, freed the state from any obligation to correct this violation. Thanks to William Phillis at the Ohio Coalition for Equity and Adequacy and to Jan Resseger of the Cleveland-based United Church of Christ and chairperson of the Committee on Public Education at the National Council of Churches, for recapitulating and updating me (January 2007) on this series of events.

153, 154   A SIMILAR SUIT FILED IN 1993 IN NEW YORK STATE: The story of this important case, *Campaign for Fiscal Equity v. State of New York,* and then-Governor George Pataki's successful obstruction of the court's decision, is documented at length in *The Shame of the Nation.* In 2006, after the state had appealed, disobeyed, and openly defied explicit orders from the court, a newly constituted court of appeals, including the new appointees of the governor, voted that although the funding levels for the children in the New York City schools were too low to meet the state's constitutional requirements, the court would nonetheless defer henceforward to the judgment of the governor and legislature as to how much money should be spent to remedy this violation. "The Legislative and Executive branches of government are in a far better position than the Judiciary to determine funding needs . . . ," according to this ruling, written by one of the governor's appointees. (*New York Post,* November 21, 2006.)

156   "I HAVE A COUPLE OF DEVIOUS PLANS" TO OBSTRUCT CLASS-SIZE AMENDMENT IF IT IS APPROVED BY VOTERS: Former Governor Jeb Bush said this "at a meeting in his office earlier this week," reported the *Gannett News Service* on October 3, 2002. After the amendment had been passed, the *St. Petersburg Times* reported (March 2, 2004) that the governor "has argued [that] the amendment is an unreasonable and costly demand by voters who didn't know what they were doing." See also *St. Petersburg Times,* December 8, 2004, and April 30, 2005.

REPUBLICAN LEGISLATORS REFUSE TO BUILD SCHOOLS AND, INSTEAD, INTRODUCE BILLS TO INCREASE THE SIZE OF CLASSES: *Palm Beach Post,* April 10, 2006.

LEGISLATORS WHO SUPPORTED AMENDMENT WERE RELUCTANT TO ANGER GOVERNOR: *Palm Beach Post,* April 10, 2006.

157   "CLASS SIZE" REDEFINED BY FLORIDA LEGISLATURE TO

278

NOTES

AVOID IMMEDIATE CONSTRUCTION OF SUFFICIENT SCHOOLS TO MEET INTENT OF THE AMENDMENT: "Under the voter-approved class-size amendment . . . , Florida classrooms must not exceed 18, 22, or 25 students," depending on grade level, notes the *Palm Beach Post* (May 17, 2006), but "with co-teaching," as approved by the legislature on May 4, 2006, "class-size numbers would be calculated using student-teacher ratios. . . . Until recently, the state Department of Education said the language of the . . . amendment prohibited districts from . . . placing two or more teachers in a classroom." But the bill passed by the legislature "would allow it." The sole constraint included in the bill is that the increased numbers of children and adults in a classroom must not break the fire codes.

FLORIDA LEGISLATORS ALLOCATE ONLY A SMALL FRACTION OF FUNDS NEEDED TO CONSTRUCT SUFFICIENT SCHOOLS: *Palm Beach Post,* May 11, 2006, and *Miami Herald,* May 30, 2006.

CLASS SIZE AS HIGH AS 32, 35, OR 40 IS COMMON IN UPPER GRADES OF MANY INNER-CITY DISTRICTS: At Walton High School in the Bronx, in the fall of 2002 (see Notes for pp. 174*ff*), I visited a math class holding 33 students. According to several students and the teacher who arranged my visit, there were many classes with enrollments ranging between 34 and 39. Across the nation, at Fremont High School in Los Angeles (see Notes for pp. 178 and 179), more than 200 classes held between 33 and 40 students when I visited in spring 2003. I spent several hours in a government class holding 40 students. The teacher had six classes every day, in which the average size was 36.

158 CLASS SIZE AT ANDOVER AND EXETER: According to their websites, Andover's average class size is 13 students, while Exeter's average class holds 12 or fewer students.

160, 161 PRINCIPAL OF THURGOOD MARSHALL SCHOOL STEERS AWAY FROM LETTING STUDENTS KNOW OF MARSHALL'S ROLE IN HISTORY: I saw a few books on Marshall in the lobby of the school, but they were in a glass case. Children I questioned were, with one exception, unaware of Marshall's participation in *Brown v. Board of Education* or, for that matter, that he was "opposed to segregation." One teacher had posted a brief summation of the *Brown* decision in an inconspicuous location in her classroom. But the resounding message

about Thurgood Marshall presented to the students in this
school, 95 percent of whom were minorities, was the one
conveyed by the "Thurgood Marshall Pledge" that empha-
sized the virtues of self-help and following instructions. For
further information on the Marshall School, see *The Shame
of the Nation.*

163 INEQUALITIES IN PER-PUPIL SPENDING IN THE NEW YORK
CITY AREA AND IN ILLINOIS: See charts and documentation
in the Appendix of *The Shame of the Nation.*

165, 166 INNER-CITY CHILDREN INCREASINGLY REQUIRED TO MAKE
CHOICES OF CAREERS WHEN THEY APPLY TO MIDDLE SCHOOL
OR HIGH SCHOOL: In *Amazing Grace* and *The Shame of the
Nation,* I describe a middle school for "Medical Careers
and Health Professions" selected by Pineapple's older sister
under the impression that this would prepare her to become a doctor. The school turned out to be one of the
city's lowest-rated middle schools and one from which only
a few students went to academic high schools and subsequently to college.

For a description of a newly established regulation in the
state of Florida that requires eighth grade students to decide on a career path when they apply to high school, which
is now in effect in Palm Beach County, see *Palm Beach Post,*
November 15, 2006. "This is intended to be a career plan
to help them better engage in making plans for their future," said Elizabeth Decker, director of curriculum for the
district, according to the *Post.* Among 53 career paths offered to the students, along with purely academic options,
were "assistant landscape technician," "sports and recre-
ational turf operation," "recreation assistant," and "military
training."

167 EXCEPTIONS TO THE PATTERN OF CAREER ACADEMIES THAT
RESTRICT THE FUTURE OPPORTUNITIES OF CHILDREN: New
York's Metropolitan Corporate Academy, created in collaboration with the Goldman Sachs investment firm, is, I am
told by teachers in New York, devoted to providing students with authentic academic preparation. This, at least,
appeared to be the case when the 98 percent black and Hispanic school began in the early 1990s. (In 2003, however,
the school enrolled 90 ninth grade students while only 55
members of the class of 2003 were still enrolled in twelfth

grade, of whom only 34 received diplomas. See Annual School Reports, New York City Public Schools, 2002–2003 and 2003–2004. In 2006–2007, according to Debbi Nagel, the school's assistant principal, there were 120 ninth graders but, again, only about 55 students who had made it to twelfth grade.) In Indianapolis, in 2006, I visited the newly founded Crispus Attucks Medical Magnet High School, in which a promising academic program that includes the study of Latin is presently in place (memo from Crispus Attucks principal Robert Faulkens, December 2006) and where, according to Pat Payne (telephone interview, November 2006), director of Multicultural Education in the Indianapolis Public Schools, there is a real commitment to prepare its students for post-secondary education. "Some of our students *will* go on to medical school," Ms. Payne is convinced.

168   CONGRESSMAN JOHN LEWIS CITED: In conversation with me, Washington, D.C., September 2003.

CHAPTER THIRTEEN: LOSS OF INNOCENCE

172, 173   EXTENDING ELEMENTARY SCHOOLS INTO THE SIXTH OR EIGHTH GRADE YEARS: Without adequate funding, however, the second of these proposals can easily shortchange the older students. In Milwaukee, for example, where K–8 schools have been begun, tight budgeting prevents these schools from hiring teachers with sufficient expertise in secondary subject areas. "One or two teachers teach all subjects in these grades," according to Bob Peterson, a Milwaukee teacher and one of the founders of *Rethinking Schools*.

174*ff*   LUNCHROOM HELL AT NEW YORK CITY HIGH SCHOOL: The school in which this experience took place is Walton High School in the Bronx. For student demographics and other documentation for this 95 percent black and Hispanic school, see *The Shame of the Nation*.

178, 179   HIGH SCHOOL IN LOS ANGELES: The school described here, Fremont High, enrolled 5,000 students on a 12-month three-track schedule, with 3,300 in attendance at a given time. For documentation and a description of my visit to the school, see *The Shame of the Nation*.

179*ff* SMALL SCHOOLS: For a fair-minded survey of small New York City high schools, see www.Insideschools.com, a project of New York–based Advocates for Children.

PLENTY OF GOOD THINGS TO BE SAID OF CERTAIN SMALL SCHOOLS: Among the best small schools I've visited, or with which I am familiar, are those begun by the Small Schools Workshop in Chicago, founded in the early 1990s by Michael and Susan Klonsky and William Ayers. One of these schools, named Telpochcalli Elementary School, which I visited in May 2006, is located in the "Little Village" neighborhood of Chicago's South Side and was begun in 1994. Although enrollment is primarily Mexican, 10 percent of students are black, and there is a small number of white students, most of whom are the children of teachers at the school: a tribute to their faith in its progressive principles.

In New York City, there are several small schools created by the nonprofit Urban Assembly, whose explicit purpose is to prepare students "for success at four-year colleges." Other promising small schools—among them, the three-year-old Bronx Academy of Letters—have been inspired or created by New Visions for Public Schools, an enlightened group that has been active in New York since the early 1990s and whose work I've followed closely in these years. (See also *New York Sun,* June 12, 2003; *New York Times,* September 19, 2003, and April 6, 2004; *Daily News,* September 9, 2003; *Newsday,* September 13, 2004; "Executive Summary," The Urban Assembly, 2006.)

With few exceptions, however (one of which is the remarkable Mission Hill School in Boston, directed until 2004 by Deborah Meier), small schools are profoundly segregated institutions and, according to Gary Orfield (see Notes for p. 77), tend to be *more* segregated even than the larger schools in urban areas. Many, too, do not enroll "problem kids" or those identified with special needs. In New York City, school department policy exempts small high schools, initially at least, from the obligation to accept such children, which artificially inflates the test scores at these schools—a policy which, intentionally or not, helps to promote the small schools concept at the expense of larger schools that are obliged to serve *all* children and where test scores are, of course, depressed accordingly.

182 SEATTLE'S MOSTLY WHITE AND UPSCALE CENTER SCHOOL:

The school, when it opened in 2001, had an 83 percent white enrollment in a city in which whites represent only 40 percent of high school students districtwide. Black enrollment was only 6 percent, although black children represent nearly a quarter of all students in the district. White enrollment declined somewhat over the next few years, leveling off at about three quarters of the students at the school by 2006, but black enrollment rose to only 9 percent. One of the very few other high schools in the city in which such a small percentage of black students are enrolled is another small school, known as Nova, which was founded decades earlier. For racial breakdowns at both these schools, see their Annual Reports for 2004, 2005, 2006, Seattle Public Schools, and "Seattle Public Schools Enrollment Count," October 2006. For further documentation of demographics at the Center School, see the school's Washington State Report Cards from 2001 to 2006.

183 NO FULL-SERVICE BOOKSTORE FOR THE 600,000 RESIDENTS OF THE SOUTH BRONX: Theodore Shaw, director-counsel of the NAACP Legal Defense and Educational Fund, who lives in the South Bronx, told me in November 2006 that in order to find a Borders, Barnes & Noble, or an independent full-service bookstore, he had to travel to the northernmost section of the Bronx that borders the adjacent suburbs or else to the Upper East Side of Manhattan. According to my close friend Anthony Bonilla, a South Bronx resident and a fanatical bibliophile since we met in his early teenage years (see *Amazing Grace*), there are "absolutely no full-service bookstores" in the area. Both Borders and Barnes & Noble confirmed to my assistant, Nayad Abrahamian, that they have no stores in the South Bronx (phone interviews, November 2006).

185 GATES FOUNDATION WEALTHIEST IN NATION: According to *Education Week* (October 11, 2006), the Gates Foundation is believed to be "the world's wealthiest private foundation."

185, 186 MY MEETING WITH TOM VANDER ARK: At the time of our meeting, Mr. Vander Ark was the Gates Foundation's executive director for education initiatives. He resigned this position in late fall 2006. Shortly before his resignation, Mr. Vander Ark told *Education Week* (October 11, 2006) that, in the aftermath of its initial focus on creating small schools, the foundation now has broadened its priorities, one of which, he said, is to help "foster an 'open sector' in education," by which he said he meant schools "outside the public . . . system." This may help explain why one of the recipients of grant support from Gates is the conservative Thomas B. Fordham Institute, one of the nation's leading advocates for privatizing education. (See *Education Week*, December 20, 2006.)

186, 187   GATES FOUNDATION PROVIDED START-UP FUNDS FOR CEN-TER SCHOOL: According to a former Seattle school official, Judy Margrath-Huge (phone interview with my assistant, Nayad Abrahamian, December 2006), who directly over-saw a $26 million grant from the Gates Foundation to the Seattle Public Schools in spring of 2000, "The Center School definitely got some money from this grant." Gates, she notes, also gave the Center School $150,000 as "a three-year start-up grant from 2000 to 2002." This informa-tion was confirmed (also in a phone interview in December 2006) by Patricia Kile, vice president for Planning and Part-nerships at the Alliance for Progress, which managed the Gates grant to the Seattle schools.

187, 188   VOLUNTARY INTEGRATION PROGRAMS GRAVELY THREAT-ENED: In December 2006, the U.S. Supreme Court heard ar-guments that challenged a voluntary integration program in Kentucky's Jefferson County, which includes Louisville and its surrounding suburbs, that had been put in place six years earlier after the termination of a mandatory program that had existed for a quarter-century. Children and parents from Louisville and other sections of the nation in which volun-tary programs have been operating with success gathered, on the day the case was heard, in front of the Supreme Court to symbolically defend these programs, which are often the sole instruments by which integration is achieved in metropolitan communities. Among those in the gathering were students from the program in the Boston area in which I taught for two years in the 1960s (see Chapter 4). In the Boston program, more than 95 percent of inner-city children who attend school in suburban districts graduate from high school, with the vast majority moving on to colleges and uni-versities. The Supreme Court's decision in the Louisville case, handed down in June 2007, ruled against the integra-tion program and, in a related case, against an integration program in Seattle's schools as well. These decisions now threaten to dismantle not only Boston's program but virtually every other voluntary integration program in the nation.

This reference to the Louisville and Seattle cases was inserted, at the time of editing, into my letter to Francesca. I have inserted similarly updated information into several of the letters where I've felt that it would be of value to the reader.

CHAPTER FOURTEEN: TEACHERS AS WITNESSES

195, 196   READING LANGSTON HUGHES TO MY FOURTH GRADERS: As a result of the incendiary racial atmosphere in Boston at the time *Death at an Early Age* was published, my publisher demanded that I reconstruct and reposition certain portions of the narrative in order to diminish the humiliation they might bring to the administrators and some teachers at my school. My publisher's purpose, as best I understood it, was to diffuse and spread the blame around as much as possible in order to present the situations I described as systematic, and not necessarily malevolent, rather than unique to a specific school or the result of racist policies enacted by my principal. I objected strongly to this fictionalizing of some portions of the narrative, but was told the book could not be published otherwise. Some of the recounting of events surrounding my reading of Langston Hughes suffered from this process of diffusion and disguise. The version of events described in this letter to Francesca is confirmed by former students as well as by notes I made at the time of my dismissal.

"A DREAM DEFERRED": See *The Collected Poems of Langston Hughes* (New York: Vintage Classics, 1995).

197   I AM FIRED FROM MY JOB: The principal did this in two stages. When I was first called to her office, there was a police officer sitting in the room who turned out to be the father of one of the very few white children in my class. He was incensed by one of the poems of Langston Hughes I'd read, and later copied for my students, in which an evicted tenant first defied his landlord, then was arrested by police. He was also angry that, among the 60 books I'd brought to class from the public library, one was about the UN Human Rights Commission. (He had, I believe,

mistaken "human rights" for "civil rights" and indicated that he felt this was unpatriotic.) The principal then told me to return to class but called me back into her office just before the schoolday ended and, at that point, told me I was fired.

198 "WE ARE TRYING TO BREAK THE SPEECH PATTERNS OF THESE CHILDREN": Marguerite Sullivan, Deputy Superintendent, Boston Public Schools, in *Boston Herald,* June 13, 1965, and *Christian Science Monitor,* June 19, 1965.

SCHOOL COMMITTEE MEMBER THOMAS EISENSTADT FINDS THAT I LACK "THE PERSONAL DISCIPLINE TO ABIDE BY RULES AND REGULATIONS": The text of his report may be found in documents appended to *Death at an Early Age.*

TEN YEARS LATER, MR. EISENSTADT IS EXPOSED FOR THEFT OF PUBLIC FUNDS: "The Boston Finance Commission in 1975 charged that then-Suffolk County Sheriff Thomas S. Eisenstadt"—he was no longer a member of the school committee at the time—"used public funds to buy fancy foods and luxury furnishings for his household," noted the *Boston Globe* (April 24, 1980) in a retrospective story. "Eventually the state moved to remove Eisenstadt from office, but rather than face court proceedings he resigned. . . . Yesterday, however, Eisenstadt was back in the news. . . . Testimony was given to a state commission that while drawing plans for a new Suffolk County jail, a Worcester architectural firm also designed a new house for Eisenstadt. . . . The cost of both projects, according to testimony, was paid by the county." See also *Boston Globe,* May 15, 1993, and September 23, 1995.

201 A WEEK LATER A MUCH LARGER PROTEST TOOK PLACE OUTSIDE OF THE BOSTON SCHOOL COMMITTEE: The protest, by this point, was no longer solely in reaction to my firing but was now directed at the full array of justified concerns the parents of black children felt, which had been symbolized and sharpened for the parents by the reasons that were given for my firing. A strong political activism in the black community, which had been stirring by that time for several years, now seemed to be dramatically intensified.

201*ff* YOUNG WHITE TEACHERS-TO-BE ARE SOMETIMES INTIMIDATED BY HEAVY-HANDED COLLEGE COURSES ABOUT "RACIAL DIFFERENCES" THAT MAKE THEM WORRY THEY WILL BE

UNWELCOME WORKING IN A BLACK COMMUNITY: Black college students, in spite of what are often very earnest efforts to recruit them, are no longer opting in large numbers to go into education; they make up scarcely 5 percent of students in our schools of education. So it does no good for anyone to load up highly principled white students who are driven by a longing to serve children of low income in our urban districts with a burden of gratuitous anxieties since they *will,* in overwhelming numbers, be the teachers of black students.

204, 205   "I'VE BEEN TO THE MOUNTAINTOP": Dr. King's final speech, delivered in Memphis, April 3, 1968, is reprinted in *A Testament of Hope: The Essential Writings and Speeches of Martin Luther King, Jr.,* ed. by James Melvin Washington (New York: HarperCollins, 1991).

CHAPTER FIFTEEN: SEEDS OF HOPE, SOURCES OF RESILIENCE

217   DEATH OF EIGHT-YEAR-OLD BERNARDO AS CONSEQUENCE OF FAULTY ELEVATOR DOOR: See *Amazing Grace* and (New York) *Daily News,* January 16, and February 4, 1994.

220   OWNER OF BERNARDO'S BUILDING, LONG HISTORY OF GROSS NEGLECT: This information was initially provided by Reverend Martha Overall, priest of St. Ann's Church, three blocks from Bernardo's building, who investigated the management of this and 37 other buildings in the neighborhood and discovered they were owned by a company called Continental Wingate, based in Massachusetts. See also (New York) *Daily News,* November 11, 1993, and February 4, 1994, and *New York Times,* March 25, 1973, and May 7, 1978.

EPILOGUE: GOODBYE FOR NOW

230*ff*   MEMORIES OF FRED ROGERS: Most of this material comes from our conversations and from the handwritten letters Mr. Rogers wrote to me in the years from 1993 to 2002. Background information on his association with Erik Erikson, the unfinished song he wrote, and the last months of his life was provided by Bill Isler, Mr. Rogers' longtime friend and his close associate in the production of *Mr. Rogers' Neighborhood.* (Conversations in March 2005, January 2007.)

MR. ROGERS IS DIAGNOSED WITH CANCER: This was in November 2002. Mr. Rogers died in February 2003.

ABOUT THE AUTHOR

JONATHAN KOZOL is the author of *Death at an Early Age, The Shame of the Nation,* and *Savage Inequalities.* He has been working with children in their inner-city schools for more than 40 years.

What Wildlife is Best Seen Where
Ratings Pertain to The Best Time To Go To Each Park Or Reserve

- ▦ **Almost Always Seen** (on most game drives)
- ▦ **Frequently Seen** (on every two–six game drives)
- ☐ **Occasionally Seen** (every one–two weeks)
- ■ **Seldom Seen** (every two–four weeks)
- ▦ **Almost Never Seen/Not Seen**

Southern Africa

Country	Park/Reserve	Lion	Leopard	Cheetah	Elephant	Black Rhino	White Rhino	Hippo	Buffalo	Eland	Greater Kudu	Sable Antelope	Gemsbok/oryx	Wild Dog	Gorillas	Chimpanzees
Botswana	Moremi/Okavango	(+)		(1)		(1)								(6)		
	Linyanti/Selinda/Kwando				(+)											
	Central Kalahari			(+)												
	Savute (Southwestern Chobe)															
	Chobe (Northern)				(+)				(+)							
	Tuli (Mashatu)		(+)		(+)											
Zimbabwe	Hwange (Makalolo/Somalisa)				(+)											
	Matusadona							(4)	(+)	(+)						
	Mana Pools				(+)				(+)							
	Malilangwe															
Zambia	South Luangwa		(2)						(+)							
	North Luangwa															
	Lower Zambezi		(2)		(+)				(+)							
	Kafue (Busanga Plains)	(5)														
	Kafue (Central)		(2)													
Namibia	Etosha															
	Ongava															
South Africa	Kruger N.P.															
	Pvt. Res. near and within Kruger	(+)	(+)(2)					(+)								
	Phinda			(+)				(+)								
	Kwandwe															

East Africa

Country	Park/Reserve	Lion	Leopard	Cheetah	Elephant	Black Rhino	White Rhino	Hippo	Buffalo	Eland	Greater Kudu	Sable Antelope	Gemsbok/oryx	Wild Dog	Gorillas	Chimpanzees
Tanzania	Lake Manyara	(5)														
	Ngorongoro	(+)												(3)		
	Serengeti (Southeastern)	(+)		(+)												
	Serengeti (Northern & Western)	(+)	(+)	(+)		(7)										
	Tarangire	(+)			(+)											
	Selous							(4)								
	Ruaha															
	Mahale/Gombe Steam															
	Katavi									(+)						
Kenya	Amboseli				(+)											
	Tsavo															
	Maasai Mara	(+)	(+)	(+)												
	Lake Nakuru															
	Samburu															
	Lewa Downs		(2)													
Uganda	Queen Elizabeth															
	Murchison Falls															
	Bwindi															
	Kibale															
Rwanda	Volcanoes N.P.															
	Nyungwe															
Congo Rep.	Odzala-Kokoua															

(+) Best Reserves
(1) Best seen in the Mombo/Chief's Island region of Moremi
(2) Seen most often on night drives
(3) In the Ngorongoro Conservation Area near Serengeti N.P.
(4) Seen more often on walks than on game drives
(5) Often seen in trees
(6) Frequently seen in the Chitabe concession
(7) Seen in the Northern Serengeti

SAFARI ACTIVITIES

Vehicles • Night Game Drives • Walking Safaris • Boat Safaris • Canoe Safaris
• Balloon Safaris • Mountain Biking • Horseback Safaris • Fishing

Southern Africa

Country	Park or Reserve	Vehicle Type Allowed			Night Drives	Walking Safaris	Boat Safaris	Canoe (C) Mokoro (M)	Balloon Safaris	Mountain Biking	Horseback Safaris	Fishing
		Open	Hatches	Closed								
Botswana	Chobe											1
	Moremi						2	M, 2				
	Okavango Delta						2	M, 2			2	
	Linyanti/Selinda/Kwando						2	C, 2				1, 2
	Savute (S.W. Chobe)											
	Central Kalahari/Nxai Pan					7						
	Tuli											
Zimbabwe	Hwange				1, 2							
	Mana Pools						1	C				
	Matusadona				1			C				
	Malilangwe							C				
Zambia	S. & N. Luangwa											
	Lower Zambezi							C, 2				
	Kafue						2		2			
Namibia	Etosha	6	6									
	Ongava											
	Damaraland									8		
South Africa	Kruger N.P.	2, 5			1, 2, 5	1, 5						
	Pvt. Reserves near and within Kruger											
	Kwandwe/Shamwari										2	
	Phinda							C				1
Mozambique	Gorongosa											
	Niassa							C				

East & Central Africa

Country	Park or Reserve	Vehicle Type Allowed			Night Drives	Walking Safaris	Boat Safaris	Canoe (C) Mokoro (M)	Balloon Safaris	Mountain Biking	Horseback Safaris	Fishing
		Open	Hatches	Closed								
Tanzania	Arusha							C				
	Lake Manyara	3			9					1		1
	Tarangire	3			1, 2	1, 2				1		
	Ngorongoro					4						
	Serengeti	3			1	1, 2						
	Selous						2					2
	Ruaha					2						
	Katavi											
	Mahale/Gombe											
Kenya	Maasai Mara	1, 3			1	1					1	
	Laikipia Reserves									2	2	2
	Samburu	1, 3				1						
	Ol Donyo Waus/Campi ya Kanzi										2	
	Amboseli/Tsavo	1, 3			1	1			1			
Uganda	Bwindi											
	Queen Elizabeth					4						
	Kibale											
	Murchison											
Rwanda	Volcanoes/Nyungwe											
Congo Rep.	Odzala-Kokoua							C, 2				

1: Activity is conducted on the outskirts of the park or reserve.
2: Activity is conducted at some camps within the reserve.
3: Open vehicles are used by some camps in the reserve.
4: Activity is conducted in certain areas of the park reserve.
5: Activity is conducted by National Parks.
6: Licensed tour operators only.
7: Walks with bushmen.
8: Operated on a group departure basis.
9: Operated by special permitted companies.

Eastern, Central and Southern Africa

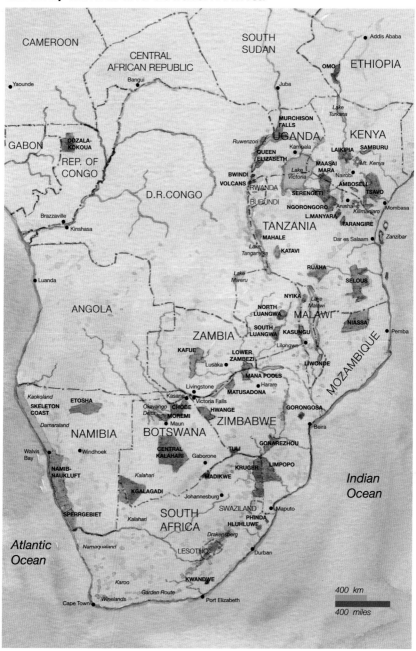

CAMEROON
Yaounde

CENTRAL AFRICAN REPUBLIC
Bangui

SOUTH SUDAN
Juba

Addis Ababa
OMO
ETHIOPIA

GABON

ODZALA-KOKOUA

REP. OF CONGO

Brazzaville

Kinshasa

D.R.CONGO

Lake Turkana

MURCHISON FALLS

Ruwenzori
UGANDA
Kampala
QUEEN ELIZABETH

BWINDI
VOLCANS
RWANDA
BURUNDI

Lake Victoria

KENYA
LAIKIPIA
SAMBURU
MAASAI MARA
Nairobi
Mt. Kenya
AMBOSELI
TSAVO
Mombasa

SERENGETI
NGORONGORO
L.MANYARA
Arusha
Kilimanjaro

TANZANIA
MAHALE

Lake Tanganyika
KATAVI

TARANGIRE
Dar es Salaam
Zanzibar

Luanda

ANGOLA

Lake Mweru

RUAHA
SELOUS

NYIKA
NORTH LUANGWA
SOUTH LUANGWA
Lake Malawi
MALAWI
NIASSA
Pemba

ZAMBIA
KAFUE
LOWER ZAMBEZI
Lusaka
KASUNGU
Lilongwe
LIWONDE

MOZAMBIQUE

Kaokoland
SKELETON COAST
ETOSHA
Damaraland

NAMIBIA

Walvis Bay

NAMIB-NAUKLUFT

Windhoek

SPERRGEBIET

Livingstone
Kasane
Victoria Falls
Okavango Delta
CHOBE
MOREMI
Maun
BOTSWANA

CENTRAL KALAHARI
Gaborone
Kalahari

KGALAGADI
Kalahari

MANA POOLS
MATUSADONA
HWANGE
ZIMBABWE

Harare
GORONGOSA
Beira

GONAREZHOU
TULI
KRUGER
LIMPOPO
MADIKWE

Johannesburg

SOUTH AFRICA

SWAZILAND
Maputo
PHINDA
HLUHLUWE
Drakensberg

Indian Ocean

Atlantic Ocean

Namaqualand

Karoo
Winelands
Cape Town

LESOTHO
Durban

KWANDWE
Garden Route
Port Elizabeth

400 km
400 miles

Southern Africa

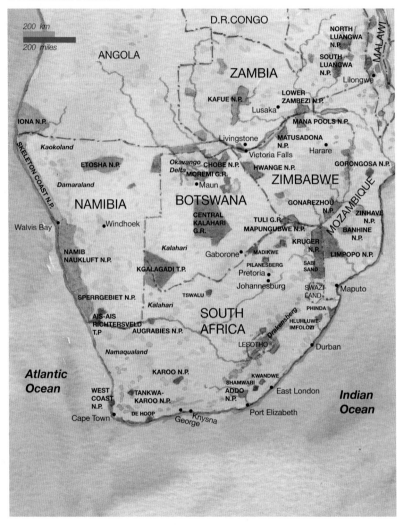

Eastern Africa

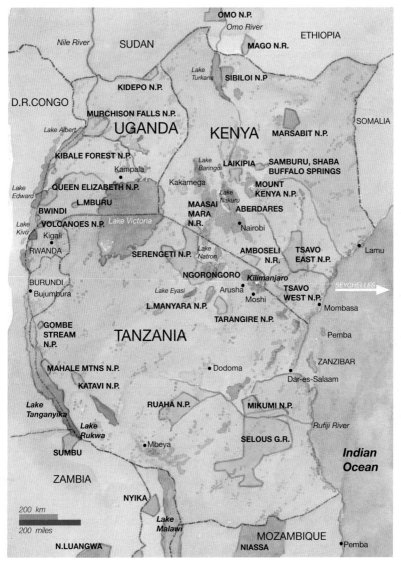

"Mark's book is an excellent tool to help you plan and make the most of a safari. I've been in Africa over 25 years and I still turn to Mark's book as a valuable resource for travel planning to the continent's greatest safari destinations."

— PATRICK BERGIN
CEO FOR AFRICAN WILDLIFE FOUNDATION

"There is no single publication available that compiles all of the truly important information one needs to prepare for a once-in-a-lifetime trip to Africa like *Africa's Top Wildlife Countries*. As someone who has been privileged to travel to that magnificent continent over 40 times, I can say without hesitation that this book is an invaluable guide to anyone planning to experience the infinite beauty and wonder of this incredible destination. Don't go on safari without reading this book first!"

— RON MAGILL
COMMUNICATIONS & MEDIA MIAMI METROZOO

"We've reached a time when safaris need to be equal parts discovery and enjoyment, wonder and excitement but also responsible and contributing to conservation, communities and making the planet better, or we will lose the very resource tourism depends on. Choosing just the right blend is difficult. Thankfully you have a great guide in the form of Mark's book. He understands quality and the excitement of Africa visited for the first time or once again. It is after all the place that philosophers and poets have gone to find inspiration."

— DERECK JOUBERT
EXPLORER IN RESIDENCE AT THE NATIONAL GEOGRAPHIC SOCIETY,
CONSERVATIONIST, FILMMAKER

"This has to be the most thorough, thoughtfully created, expertly written guidebook on the region. It includes everything that every type of traveler wants and needs to know...With Mark Nolting's guidebook, there are no questions left unanswered, and no subjects unexplored. Mr. Nolting really is the leading expert on African travel, and he captures the nuances, details, facts, figures, and images of South Africa so perfectly here. Reading this brought me right back to my life-changing journey through Southern Africa, as planned by the Africa Adventure Company, and made me eager to return."

— PAMELA JACOBS
FORMER EDITOR-IN-CHIEF OF NY RESIDENT MAGAZINE

"An incredible resource for anyone looking to experience the magic of an African safari. From in-depth descriptions of Africa's national parks and must-do activities to the perfect time of year for animal viewing, the information provided is clear and concise. A wonderful guide to help anyone plan the trip of a lifetime."

— LISA LOVERRO
AFRICA AND MIDDLE EAST CORRESPONDENT FOR
JAX FAX TRAVEL MARKETING MAGAZINE